EVERYTHING I LEAVE
BEHIND FOR YOU

thank you! :)
- emily

hope thang
:) gabriel

EVERYTHING I LEAVE BEHIND FOR YOU

Emily Her

NEW DEGREE PRESS
COPYRIGHT © 2022 EMILY HER
All rights reserved.

EVERYTHING I LEAVE BEHIND FOR YOU

ISBN
979-8-88504-081-5 *Paperback*
979-8-88504-710-4 *Kindle Ebook*
979-8-88504-189-8 *Digital Ebook*

Dedication-ish

3:09 a.m. Thank you all for being people whose trustworthiness I don't need to ever question. I know I've seen a lot in this world. I've been through a lot. **I know I should have been broken down and battered away until I could no longer hold anything but apathy and disdain for humanity, but, because of you, I still have hope.** *Because of you, I still choose to take risks and trust and open myself.* **I know I have been unlucky in so much of my past, but I know that the luckiest thing that has happened to me is all of you.** *Thank you all. I hope you also trust me the way I trust you.*

"Are you happy now?"

"I'm happy.

"You were so sad earlier."

"Maybe [you're] a little broken but definitely not beyond fixing."

3:16 a.m. Thank you all. That is all I can say. Thank you.

CONTENTS

PART I   **11**
INTRODUCTION-ISH   13
AUTHOR'S NOTE-ISH   17
(THIS IS NOT A) MEMOIR-ISH   25
(THIS IS ALSO NOT A) BOOK-ISH   33
INSTRUCTIONS-ISH   37

PART II   **41**
DAILY REMINDERS   43

PART III   **65**
VULNERABLE   67
UNANSWERED QUESTIONS   75
IDENTIFIED PROBLEMS   79
HEALING   91
CHILDHOOD   99
ACCOUNTABILITY   115
CONTROL   121
HOME   129

BOUNDARIES	135
COPING MECHANISMS	145
LOVELESS	153
OPTIMIZATION	167
FEAR OF DEATH	177
THERAPY	185
PRODUCTIVITY	195
FRIENDS	207
ACTS OF KINDNESS	213
IDENTITY	223
FORGIVENESS	231
PERMISSION	237
HOPE	249
PART IV	**259**
A LETTER	261
ACKNOWLEDGMENTS	265

Epigraph-ish

#365. Get used to feeling happy.
Get used to things working out.

[Docile Dreams]

To hesitate is to make waste
of streetlights lit so soon.
To roll and slumber in docile dreams
of nightmares merrily unknown,
floating on fragile beds
of dainty, silly things.

PART I

HOW ARE YOU

INTRODUCTION-ISH

Hey, how are you? How is your day?

What are you up to today?

How human are you feeling today? Did you remember to check in on yourself today?

When was the last time you talked with yourself? When did you look at yourself in the mirror and memorize everything that makes up that beautiful face?

Did you recently pause for a moment when you caught yourself smiling? What made you smile?

When was the last time you talked to someone else? When did you last check in on someone and ask how their day was? How their day *really* was? When did you last share a moment or a smile with another human?

What if we could be vulnerable with each other? What if, for a day, we had one less wall around our hearts? How would we interact if we were all just a little bit more transparent about our thoughts?

What are some of the hard questions you are not asking yourself? Are you avoiding these questions, or simply waiting for someone else to answer them? Are you scared of their answers? Where are the answers hidden inside of you? Why are you not answering those hard questions?

What was the last meaningful connection you made with another person? How did it begin? Do you wish you knew them earlier than you did? What is stopping you from connecting with them again?

What kind of world do you think we would have if we were all a bit more human to each other? What if we got to know each other's stories just a little bit more? And what if we were to recognize that underneath all of those layers, we are more similar inside than we thought?

How often do you let yourself be present? When were you present in *the present*, not caught in the past or trying to keep up with the future? Why are you not present with yourself right now? What is stopping you?

Do you owe yourself a checkup? What is going on inside of your head and your heart? How close do you let the two of them get to each other? Why are they not closer?

How are you feeling? What are you thinking about, and what are you scared of? What are you hoping for and what are you doubting? Would today be a fulfilling last day in this world? What would you do to make it one?

How are you?

AUTHOR'S NOTE-ISH

At eleven, I promised myself I would not live past sixteen. At sixteen, I was held in a mental hospital after my third attempted suicide. At twenty-one, I graduated from the University of Chicago.

During my freshman year of college, I was told that continuing my education jeopardized my survival given how much danger I was putting my body in. I struggled with depression, anxiety, and eating disorders since I was eleven. My struggles threatened not just my academics but also my literal heart. By refusing to drop out of school for inpatient care, I risked my life at my own hands. Unfortunately, I am only one of millions who struggle daily to simply live with myself.

But I also am one of millions who refuse to just be a statistic.

I am often asked what drives me to keep living during the darkest hours. I used to be lost for an answer and temporarily found security in saying it was all for a stable future. This wasn't a complete lie—hope was my greatest weapon I did not know I had. However, I now know my will to live and fight is driven by the wish to help as many people as I can to never experience the depths I have experienced.

I was born and raised in Northern California. As a child, I spent most of my time in a small town within the East Bay and Silicon Valley areas. My family was lower-middle class, but I attended public schools where most students came from families better off than my own—a disparity obvious to me early on. Both of my parents are present in my life, as well as a brother two years older than me. My father made most of the income as a software engineer while my mother cared for the children, teaching at weekend Chinese schools. They both immigrated from Taiwan, so our household was heavily traditional to their native culture.

The community I grew up in was majority Asian (slightly over 80 percent the last time I checked). The environment was competitive, with our schools ranking within the top 100 in the country despite being public schools. Put bluntly, the culture was toxic: parents compared students, and children were pushed to their limits but could never be seen as good enough in their own eyes. Overwhelming emphasis was placed on academics as our sole priority. Our school was less than ten years old yet already competitive on national levels.

I felt immense pressure from my family and community to be the best. My family was unable to afford expensive after-school tutors or programs like many of my friends could, so I spent much of my time studying by myself to keep up with them. I excelled in schoolwork from a young age, but with that came a feeling that the better I performed, the more pressure and expectations were thrown on me. My middle school years were difficult. I was first diagnosed with depression and anxiety at twelve after my first suicide attempt was made, but this was already after months of self-harm habits and my first experience with sexual assault. Along with my parents fighting regularly, they did not believe I was mentally struggling because of the way they were raised in Taiwan. Life at home became worse when they accused me of faking how I felt. I closed myself off from the world even more.

In high school, my condition worsened as the culture became increasingly toxic and my family life nonexistent. At this point, I barely told my parents anything about myself, shutting my door for hours of studying and work time. I developed an unhealthy obsession with wanting to always be productive. I cried myself to sleep and was scared of returning to the house after school. Running away at night to escape into the dark evening was commonplace. Anxiety attacks struck me regularly, making me faint during school days or scream and cry endlessly in my dark room for hours. I had unhealthy relationships with boyfriends as temporary means to escape from reality as I was unstable more often than not. I lost count of the number of suicide attempts I made, blurring the lines between when self-harm was fatal enough to be considered "suicidal." After one particular overdose, the police were called on me by a few friends, and I found myself transferred from ambulance to hospital to mental hospital. I was held for a few weeks before returning to school. Before my graduation, I was raped for the first time.

Despite all the inner turmoil I faced, I always kept a smile on at school. I did not allow any of my home life to be apparent when I showed up every morning to first period, even graduating from my high school as the speaker at our graduation ceremony.

I was basically living a double life.

I moved to Chicago for college, where I continued to excel in academics. While I made new friends and enjoyed my time away from California, my issues unfortunately did not leave me alone. I dedicated myself to graduating a year early, overloading my class schedule in sacrifice of my well-being. Unbeknown to me, I brought along a budding eating disorder that manifested itself as anorexia. In my first year, I was hospitalized and serious considerations were made for me to drop out of school since my health was hanging on a thread. I remember nights of cold shocks, heartbeats thumping in my ears, and an inability to control my breathing as I curled up underneath blankets in fear of whether I would wake up the next day. Throughout this time, I was in a toxic relationship that reinforced much of the pressure I tried to leave in California. My mental disorders continued to hurt me for years in Chicago as I struggled to cope with their existence. Suicide attempts, rape, and toxic behavior reappeared.

Right before graduation at twenty, I hit financial crisis. Due to family matters, my immunocompromised health, and irrational choices, the six-figure savings account I diligently built up for years was gone in a matter of months. On top of my course load, I was working five to six internships and part-time serving to save up as much as I could. It felt like all of the sacrifices I'd made were now surmounting to nothing. Years of labor, tears, and dedication were taken away from me. I never attended a single social event in high school or college once I began full-time serving—and eventually working as an assistant manager—at a local restaurant when I turned sixteen. I gave up opportunities of happiness for opportunities to work. You do not know what it feels like when all you've worked for your whole life is suddenly reduced to nothing until it happens to you.

I graduated at twenty-one and began to work full time. My family life was a mess of loose ends and cut ties I never resolved, and it began to catch up with me, consistently haunting me. I was diagnosed with complex post-traumatic stress disorder (CPTSD), borderline personality disorder (BPD), and obsessive-compulsive personality disorder (OCPD). I began seeing three therapists but still struggled to be okay with my own existence.

As I am writing now, I am six months out from my graduation. I tried my hardest to stay alive for these last twenty-one years, having come close to the edge more often than I would like to keep track. After my first suicide attempt at eleven, I told myself I would not let myself live past sixteen. I did not have any real reason for why I chose sixteen. I suppose I wanted to live long enough to experience life, yet not long enough to experience a hard life. I did not want to be a part of this cruel world anymore.

Waking up every day is hard when you are scared of waking up every day. Yet, I still did.

The fact that my life has seen multiple lows does not mean I never saw a high. I shake my head when asked if I would ever live my life differently. While I would never wish my life on others, I also would not wish for it to be different. I know life will continue to barrage me with obstacles I cannot fathom yet. I cannot promise myself I will always be okay. Since I learned so much through each of my struggles, I want to promise myself I will always continue to grow. My story is not over yet, and the chapters I already crossed will be what guide me from here. The rest of this book will be the journal of those chapters.

I am not trying to tell a good story—just my story. And maybe part of it is your story too.

For the past year and a half I've been writing my book, *Everything I Leave Behind for You*. For years, I've asked myself how and when I could share my story. When I found myself struggling again this past year, I found my answer: the time to help others is always now.

My hope is that my writing will give readers a greater determination to recognize the human in all of us, even in those whose stories we may never know. I hope it encourages you to live life with a little bit more purpose and a little bit more compassion. No matter what we crumple under, are stumbling over, or will be beaten by, we cannot wait for the world and its challenges to pass by before we take charge of our own lives and happiness. Through my book, I collect memories from conversations, the mental hospital, and therapy in a raw and vulnerable expression of my struggles so others will make choices guided by my experiences.

I hope we can all find the will to find ourselves. We are all a little bit lost, after all.

AUGUST 6

5:50 p.m. Yesterday, you told me I have a knack for making new people feel comfortable opening up to me, and I told you I believe I have just been fortunate to have met so many amazing people in my life with colorful and fulfilling life stories. You told me it was actually something within me that makes people talk to me easily. I brought this question to my therapist today. We discussed it and he asked me how much I believe in your statement. I said roughly 15-20 percent, and he asked me why not 100 percent. I responded by saying this was the same recurring topic we had gone over many times already, that I know I doubt myself and discount many of my characteristics. A part of me may believe that because I am so open about my story, others feel comfortable to do so as well. But it's just hard for me to credit myself for anything. It's just . . . who I am. It's what I'm working on. I promise. In the meantime, thank you to everyone who has been trusting me and continues to trust me. Your trust in me gives me strength in myself and my capability to help you. Thank you.

THERE IS A
GARDEN GROWING
IN MY HEAD AND I
WANT TO SHARE
THESE FLOWERS
WITH YOU

(THIS IS NOT A) MEMOIR-ISH

There is a garden growing in my head and I want to share these flowers with you. What is beautiful in this world is only beautiful when it can be appreciated with others.

I am less than qualified to be writing this book. I never won any awards for my subpar writing skills and never studied counseling. Nonetheless, I was told by various individuals in my life that I should write a book about my story and that I should share my story with others to motivate, inspire, and comfort. Even my therapist mentioned that my story is worth sharing with the world. It took over ten sessions for me to explain my life to him when we were first introduced. At the end of it all, he paused to comment that throughout his decades of therapy, he has never met someone who carries as much poison as I do, much less at my age.

I am no celebrity. My life has generally not been the most exciting to read about (much less for me to write about), so I will save you from that.

I began this book expecting to write my story. I planned to share a memoir of sorts, detailing experiences through struggles and healing alike. After writing a few pages, I noticed I was spending more time and words on my healing and my thoughts throughout that process. I always say I go where the wind takes me, and it seems the wind was giving me a different direction. I decided I would instead dedicate this book to walking my readers through the many forms of help, support, and conversations that contributed to my healing. I believe this will be a better use of your time too.

I am writing this book to ask the world to be a bit more human with itself.

I hope as you read you find yourself reflected in my writing. We may not share the same experiences or thoughts, but take this as a sort of journal that records my healing for you. I hope this book helps untangle you from knots you did not recognize in yourself. You do not need to have the same struggles as I do; you do not even need to be in a place of struggle. I believe no matter who we are or where we are in our lives, we can always benefit from thinking, reflection, and introspection.

My life has been surrounded by help and support due to problems overwhelming my daily life. Whether I accepted or was receptive to this help is a different conversation, but I was fortunate enough to have resources and individuals whose presence taught me how to live. I hope I can share the most important details and lessons I have collected, delivering to you what I learned from difficult experiences. I hope you do not need to go through what I have in order to live the path of growth to becoming more human.

Here's what this book is not:

- **A medically approved guidebook.** I am not medically trained at all (I took as few science classes as I could in school). This book is meant to share my experiences, thoughts, interactions, and learnings, but is by no means meant to be used as a source of certified truth. It is, however, a source of truth of an individual's growth.

- **A profiling reference.** While there are definitely many individuals who share the same disorders, upbringings, thoughts, and characteristics as me, this does not mean they are me. This book is not meant to be a resource to generalize individuals who walked similar paths of life as mine. We experience our lives in completely different ways from one another and deserve respect for the individual stories we carry.

- **A final work.** I am always working on myself, and this book was written at a point when I made significant progress. By no means are these writings meant to show "end goals" or "final destinations"; instead, they should be used as catalysts for new perspectives in thinking and consideration for one another.

Here's what this book is:
- **A conversation starter.** I hope this book starts much-needed and overdue conversations with both yourself and others. Each topic is the condensed result of constant discussion with therapists, friends, strangers, and myself. Let them be guiding points if you find yourself having thoughts that deserve headspace.

- **A single data point.** My experiences are a single data point in a sea of endless generations and stories. Just one. But like all of ours, mine is still a data point. Therefore, while I am not asking you to take what I write as a Holy Grail, I am also not asking you to take what I write to be worthless of consideration. I am but another voice in multiple conversations you will have around these topics. Allow me to be a voice present in the room.

- **A safe space.** I may or may not know you, and you may or may not know me. Nonetheless, I hope the candor and transparency in my writing will show one person at a time they are less alone than they think. I find it such a pity when we are unable to feel like ourselves because those around us feel more like strangers than humans. Let this book be a place where you can feel safe to be you.

- **An invitation to be more human.** If you find this book stirring up emotions and feelings, then let them be stirred. I hope more and more people can recognize the humanity in themselves, which they may not always take time to consider. One book alone cannot cover everything that makes us who we are, but it can get us thinking.

- **A connection with more humans.** To a certain extent, I hope you do not relate to everything I write about. Maybe you will find yourself in a few places and find someone else you know in others. If you come across someone you know in these writings, let reading this be a step toward starting a conversation and hearing their perspective. Mental disorders and conversations in our heads are not easy to explain in compact terms but can be better understood when we share how our minds work.

- **A selfish project of my own.** I know I tend to be a very happy, talkative, and loud individual, yet I was not always very honest about the voices in my head or the struggles in my heart. I showed the world a happy-go-lucky smile while, inside my room, I cried myself to sleep. Even with my closest friends and loved ones, I still bend truths. Even when I opened up about my pain, I only showed the tip of the iceberg while so much hurt hid underneath. Unable to open up completely to others in my life meant I was dishonest, even with myself. I recognized only recently how many dark thoughts and traumas I myself was not able to face. I hope that by being honest with my struggles and my healing with you I can also become more honest with myself.

- **A reminder to myself.** On my harder days, when I am a bit more lost, maybe these pages can guide me back.

I will always be growing and healing through growth. This is an open invitation for you, my reader, to grow with me. Let us return to humanity.

PURPOSE IN LIFE

JULY 10

5:30 p.m. When you ask me what my purpose in life is or what I find meaning in, I find my answer is to make others happy. I don't know when this distorted into a reliance on others. In the mental hospital for inpatient care in high school, the first time I ever cried for someone was when I saw her incredibly happy to be reunited with her family. When she later told me I was the reason she was able to persevere for so long and eventually be as happy as she was, I felt a happiness I had never felt before. When another patient told me the same thing—that he was able to stay positive because I had been by his side—I had the same feeling. When friends and strangers seeking comfort come to me with stories, experiences, and secrets, I feel myself filled with that same happiness. **I want to be** *open about the experiences I've had so I can be a safe space for others. I don't want anyone to ever experience what I did.* If I can be part of what stops them from reaching that point, then that is all I ask for. Even though I may be busy with work, I would drop anything to support my friends and be by their side. The potential magnitude of support I can provide them in a dark time means much more than any work I could be occupied with. I guess this desire to help people is what made me begin to rely on others for my happiness. My happiness relies on their happiness, while my depression is a function of my own blame and guilt.

11:46 p.m. I was reminded again of why I am writing this journal. **I completely believe that verbalizing or writing down thoughts makes them that much more real, tangible, and part of this world.** They no longer have the chance to be erased with a mere distraction. I guess I'm hoping that bringing these thoughts into the world will finally allow me to be truthful, especially to myself. It's strange; it feels like I'm writing simply to know myself better. Maybe I am. What does that say about how I have been living and how I have perceived myself? I'm not currently strong enough to reread my journal. So many ugly truths were written every day. I am not strong enough to revisit them yet, but one step at a time I'm putting them out into the world, making myself acknowledge and realize my dark secrets. I hope one day I will be strong enough to not only revisit and reread this journal, but to turn it into a part of who I am.

"I know things are hard right now and you're going through so much, and I know you might think there's no way around this, but things are going to get better. You've probably heard this about a *thousand times and you're sick of it, but life can't be like this forever. One day, all your problems are going to fade away. All these things you worry about now aren't going to mean anything as time passes. You will get better, and I'm not saying you won't have to face more problems later on, because you probably will. But there will always be a solution. Please don't hurt yourself and please don't kill yourself. Someone loves you more than you think, even if you don't know it. Focus on the people who listen to you, not on those who hurt you. Surround yourself by positivity and don't give up. Keep standing tall and just know that sometimes it's okay to fall apart. It's okay to cry and let everything out. You're only human, and breaking down doesn't make you weak. Sometimes we just need to remind ourselves of that. I hope in a few years you'll wake up with a smile on your face, and you'll have forgotten about everything that has been holding you back. I hope that you'll be able to smile a real smile again and know everything is okay, and I hope you'll feel happy again. Please don't give up. Please don't lose hope."*

(THIS IS ALSO NOT A) BOOK-ISH

Do I need this book?

The short answer is no. Chances are, your life will continue to carry on as it previously has.

If you will indulge me, the long answer is . . .

I never believed in reading self-help books.

My therapist recommended countless books to me to start my healing and I always brushed them off as unnecessary. I processed the world better with dynamic conversations instead of books with static words on pages. I never read these books, always averting eye contact when my therapist asked again and again if I had read his recommendations yet.

I did not begin reading self-help books until I was gifted one by a mentor, and during a slow shift at work this book just happened to be lying in the dusty bottom of my backpack. I gave it a try to pass the time (after all, there was only so much online shopping I could do in a day).

How did my view of self-help books change? Well, somehow, I am now an author of one.

I cannot promise that by reading this book your world will be changed and you will be a better person (by whatever subjective definition you use). You may not come out of reading this completely healed from your past or ongoing struggles. I do not have that kind of power, despite how much I wish I did.

If you do read this book, I only ask that you remain as open-minded as possible throughout. Look for places where you can find yourself reflected in the writings. Keep the thoughts of my mind in your mind as you move forward in your life.

Some of us struggle a bit more with ourselves than others do. Some of us love ourselves a bit more than others do. Yet all of us are human, and we can always find a bit more of that humanity in ourselves.

I was unable to begin my healing for over a decade since I was transfixed on my own worldview, absolutely unmoving in how I saw myself and my place in this life. I was unable to let myself see how human it was for me to be in pain and how human it was to not be a robot. I am not perfect and still learning more about me, but that is what makes me human. It took conversations, struggles, and many, many patient people to open my eyes and help me see how much I did not know about myself. I want to help you talk to the human inside of you too.

However, the truth is that this is not a self-help book. It *can* be a self-help book, but this is a book of conversation starters. Those conversations could be with friends, partners, family, strangers, or yourself.

I do not know your story and neither does the person sitting next to you on the train during your 5:00 p.m. commute home. We will never have enough time to know the stories of every single person we interact with. One thing is certain: we each experience our stories as living characters. I do not have the answers to where your story will go from here, but that is not my intention. Instead, I hope that with this book you can recognize the stories we all experience in our lives so you might be a bit more empathetic to the person sitting next to you on the train during your 5:00 p.m. commute home.

INSTRUCTIONS-ISH

This book is a compilation of my thoughts, one after the other. I recommend the book be approached in the order in which it has been presented, but reading out of order can also create different thought processes as you get to know its content in varying sequences. Like a stream of consciousness, there is no true chronological order to these writings. The chapters can be read as separate from each other and can develop their own conversations. However, when they are put in conversation with each other, the real discussions begin.

In other words, do with these what makes the most sense to you.

Each chapter will begin with a short thought from the first chapter, "Daily Reminders." Let it guide the start of each conversation.

Many chapters will include italicized snippets of my journal. Directly taken from my daily writings, my words are as raw and unfiltered as when they were first felt. Allow this book to share intimate insights into how a human thinks and where their mind goes. Let it be a thorough introspection of another human's existence to encourage more human interactions, understanding, and sympathy.

This book is nothing more or less than an unadulterated, unglamorized recollection of thoughts from when my mind was running faster than I could keep up.

PART II

DAILY REMINDERS

Reminders for each day of the year to help you remember we're all human on the inside.
1. You have been doing the best you can with the information you have. You couldn't have done anything more.
2. You are not the same person today as you were a year ago, and you should be proud of that.
3. This life is not a bad life; today is just a bad day.
4. Don't let bad people stop you from being a good person.
5. You're allowed to enjoy your day even if it's not perfect.
6. Remember how it feels when you feel like you are at your best.
7. It would be so much easier if I could tell you that things get better, but they don't. Instead, you get stronger in a world that is trying to hold you down.
8. Keep people in your life who know how to wait when you need time to heal.
9. You don't need to impress anyone with your life choices other than the last version of you.
10. It is okay to let it hurt but remember to also let it heal and then let it go for good
11. Don't light yourself on fire to keep others around you warm.

12. If you woke up again this morning, then it means that your story is not done yet.
13. Do your best to be kind to someone every day, but do not forget that you are also a someone.
14. Be the best person that you can be, but don't waste time trying to prove your worth to anyone who can't see it already.
15. Life is tough. You are tougher.
16. But you tried, didn't you? And that's all that should matter.
17. You don't get to bloom until you water yourself.
18. If the people around you make you feel selfish for prioritizing your safety and peace, then so be it.
19. Do it for the people you haven't met who will love you the way you love yourself.
20. The only closure you need is knowing that you tried your best.
21. It's okay to be quiet.
22. You deserve healthy love from everyone, starting with yourself.
23. If it's right, then you won't need to force it to happen.
24. You can apologize for your mistakes, but you cannot apologize for your feelings.
25. Growth can sometimes feel like loss.
26. Progress is still progress, no matter how small it may seem today.
27. Let go of that person you used to be. You aren't that person anymore, and you need to give yourself grace.
28. All we can control in our lives is our mindset going into anything. Don't try to control what you cannot reach.
29. Shift your attention to what you like about your life before being consumed with what you hate.

30. Don't let yourself feel small.
31. Being anxious makes you live things twice, and that's already two times too many.
32. Progress is not linear: it staggers, comes fast or slow, and comes in loops. All that matters is that it moves forward.
33. Recovery is easier in retrospect, when you can only see what's behind you. The future is there if you look forward.
34. Offer others the grace of being empathetic; we don't know each other's stories.
35. Instead of apologizing, thank others for their patience and kindness.
36. Hearts are not built to be deflated.
37. Give your heart the safe space in the presence of people who will respect your story and vulnerability.
38. Today is a good day to begin the story you want to live.
39. Temporary Band-Aids are okay as long as they are just temporary.
40. Are you truly working toward happiness, or just running from what you fear?
41. Don't compare your inside to others' outsides.
42. Love yourself enough to know when enough is enough.
43. Missing who you were is okay, but know when it's time to say goodbye.
44. Don't take the world for granted. You are a part of the world too.
45. You deserve the most love when you feel the least lovable.
46. Congratulations on breaking up with the unhealthy parts of you.
47. Are your boundaries set where you need them to be?

48. It won't make sense all the time, but it'll always be okay.
49. Be healed, not distracted.
50. Once you've finished your part, close the chapter and let go.
51. Will you be there for yourself like you want everyone else to be?
52. Trying to be liked by everybody is especially pointless when you don't even like everybody.
53. Just because it comes back to you does not mean you need to let it back in.
54. The conversations worth having with yourself are the hardest ones to start.
55. Your instincts reflect your fears, not who you are. Reflect on your thoughts, not your instincts.
56. Be grateful for those who walk into your life, and even more grateful for those you've walked away from.
57. You do not have enough time in this world to be dropping hints about what you need. Speak your boundaries.
58. Is what you're holding on to driving you forward or driving you down?
59. I wish I were obsessed with myself. I wonder, what is with our generation's thing for self-deprecation?
60. You're the only person who needs to spend 100 percent of your life with yourself. The difference between your friends, your family, and you is that they can walk away at any point, but you can't.
61. I might cry all the time, yet I still get things done.
62. What if it does all work out in the end?
63. Your worth is not defined by your productivity.
64. A past version of you is proud of where you are now, and you'll be proud of a future version of you too.

65. You're not missing out on anything good if you're taking time to make yourself greater.
66. Do not undervalue what you are by overvaluing what you are not.
67. What if I fall? But what if I fly?
68. Take the time you need to heal your inner child.
69. Too much happens in life. Don't forget to love yourself first amid all of it.
70. Slow healing deserves your celebration too.
71. Don't let your empathy come before your self-respect.
72. Make peace with what didn't happen instead of waging war with what did.
73. One day, you will feel the blue sky and warm sunlight in your heart. Can you make that day today?
74. A part of me is an optimistic hopeless romantic, and the other part of me is a pessimistic, damning realist. Both are beautiful just the way they are.
75. Make this a life worth living.
76. Is what you're holding on to the best use of the space it's taking up?
77. I want to be so grounded in myself that even the unknown terrors cannot shake me.
78. Sometimes you're the one being toxic to yourself. It's not you, but the parts of yourself that you need to let go of.
79. Know when to stop.
80. Tough times will not be permanent, but tough people will be.
81. Fall once again, and get up once more.
82. You cannot heal in the same environment that hurt you in the first place.
83. We all have a chapter in our book that we don't read out loud, but it still makes up a part of our story.

84. You didn't fight so hard to come this far to have come only this far.
85. We are as blind as we let ourselves be to the lights around us.
86. If you haven't found what you're looking for, then maybe it's because something greater is looking for you.
87. You are allowed to change your mind about what you want to keep and discard in your life. Everything is only as permanent as you let it be.
88. The day you realize you do not have to prove your worth to anyone, including yourself, will be the day you break free.
89. No one deserves the bad things that happen to them, and that includes you.
90. You don't owe anyone an explanation for your bad days.
91. Find the strength to forgive yourself when you are closest to giving up.
92. Just because no one sees your progress does not mean you are not making progress.
93. All that matters anymore is that you're still trying.
94. Our real tests come when we are faced with the hardest challenges. Make sure you are ready for them.
95. The waves will always pass with time, as long as you are not swept up in their flow.
96. You're too good to be bad to yourself.
97. Be the reason that someone else can believe in good people today.
98. Taking longer than others does not mean you failed but that you took the time to smell the flowers along the way.
99. Have you reminded yourself that you have survived everything you thought you wouldn't?

100. Yet we grow.
101. If you've been judging yourself for years, have you considered accepting yourself?
102. Let every situation be what it is instead of thinking of what it should be.
103. You're not overreacting when you are hurt. Pain is pain.
104. Our good days are here because our bad days let us know what they look like.
105. Care for yourself more when you are quietest.
106. Love does not hurt you, but people who do not know how to properly love you will hurt you. Start with loving yourself.
107. The happiest you've ever been will only be a fraction of the happiest you will ever be. You owe yourself the biggest apology for putting up with what you did not deserve.
108. Maybe you aren't getting what you want out of the world because the world knows you deserve better.
109. You can't protect your heart by acting like you hate it.
110. You are your permanent home. Start taking care of your home.
111. You can put your life on pause until you are ready to return to it again. It'll be here for you.
112. When you look back on your life one day, be glad you chose it instead of settling on it.
113. Treat yourself the way you treat others.
114. Unlearning trauma also means unlearning the survival tactics that shaped who you became. Give yourself grace and patience.
115. Pain builds walls for us. Healing finds the doors in those walls.

116. No one in this world is judging you as hard as you are judging yourself.
117. The grass is greenest where you water it.
118. Your life is less yours the more you care about what others think.
119. Flowers and rainbows are both beautiful, yet they look very different. Stop comparing your light with that of others.
120. Someday, the happiest version of you will be glad you did not give up.
121. Everything in life begins one step at a time. Then another. And then another.
122. There's no guarantee that it will always work out, but the adventure you'll have will be worth that answer.
123. You can't make the world love you by giving it more of what it refuses to love.
124. The moment you begin to wonder if you deserve better is the moment that you give yourself better.
125. If you wait your whole life for the storm to pass, then you will never learn to dance in the rain.
126. Would you want to be friends with people who treat you the way you treat yourself?
127. It's okay if you're not where you want to be in life. Sometimes the detours are just taking us back on track.
128. Your perfect future does not require you to have a perfect past, so stop holding yourself back.
129. It's never too late to chase a new dream.
130. The trees do not know the rest of the forest, but they all reach for the same sun.
131. This is not who you are. This is who you became as a result of your traumas.

132. Burn the bridges if doing so will stop you from crossing them again.
133. You deserve to celebrate who you fought not to be.
134. Your worst enemy is your own memories when you let them consume you.
135. You don't need to be perfect to deserve happiness.
136. Some chapters do not have an ending because not knowing is better than chasing an answer you do not need.
137. One day, you will be strong enough to face it all even if it does not feel like that day is today.
138. Realize the superhero you've been looking for is you.
139. Every hard ending is a disguise for a beautiful beginning.
140. The hardest thing you can do is give yourself the permission to become who you want to be.
141. The worst days only have twenty-four hours over you.
142. Today is a good day to make yourself glow.
143. Nothing in your life will ever go away until you've learned what it was meant to teach you.
144. You don't need to be perfect; all you need to be is a better version of yourself.
145. Be your biggest fan because you're the only one directing your spotlight.
146. Would you like this version of you if you met yourself?
147. Save yourself before you save others. Every airplane teaches you that for the emergency evacuation.
148. Have you realized that you have already walked through doors you never thought would open?
149. Think about yourself in your highest place and realize you are already on the path there.

150. The person who will change your life most is the one you see in the mirror. It's about time you got to know them.
151. How many times do you need to look in the mirror to realize how much of a blessing it is that you are still in this world?
152. Do not ever feel bad for doing what is best for you.
153. You do not need to have it all figured out right now. Go to sleep, and you can figure it out tomorrow.
154. The hardest goodbyes will make for the easiest hellos.
155. Change the memories and laugh where the last version of you died.
156. Your happiness does not need to make sense to others to be valid.
157. You're the writer of your own story; you can include all the plot twists and character development you want.
158. You're still a winner if you lost someone but found yourself.
159. I can be strong and soft. I can be independent and need support.
160. It's okay to not be okay. Nonetheless, you will be okay.
161. If you are putting yourself last, then that relationship was not meant to last.
162. You can't flip the next page of your story if you are stuck rereading the last one.
163. What if you already have the keys but just have not found the right doors? Stop trying to break down the ones that won't open.
164. You deserve more than the bare minimum from the world and yourself.
165. You've done so well with so little. You can do anything with everything now.

166. There is nothing wrong with you. You are trying your best to exist in an environment that does not support your best.
167. The future has already begun. Stop waiting for it to come, and start living its arrival.
168. You can't change the people around you, but you can change the people who surround you.
169. Have a crush on yourself like you're still in middle school.
170. Be the reason your heart smiles today.
171. Life is made up of the small moments. Live them with gratitude.
172. What if all we had left was now?
173. Imperfections are perfections that have not had time to grow.
174. No footstep stays in place forever. Let go of what has already let go of you.
175. You are enough.
176. It's not cool to try to play it cool when everything is not cool.
177. You deserve more than people who are not sure about you.
178. The world is only what you make of it, so express more about your joys than your problems.
179. Isolation might just be the gift you need for yourself. Learn how to be alone.
180. Dream so hard that your dream becomes your reality.
181. Look with gratitude for what is there instead of looking for what isn't.
182. Never be so caught up in making a living that you sacrifice making a life.
183. Celebrate your own wins. No one else will know what it took to reach them.

184. "Doing your best" means doing your best with your mental health too.
185. If you keep pretending you are not hurt, you will never begin to heal.
186. Love yourself before loving the idea of others loving you.
187. Our greatest progress is often what we are most blind to.
188. You will never be able to give your life more time, so give the time you have left more life.
189. Give yourself the world that you deserve.
190. There will always be another person who does not see your worth. Don't let that person be you.
191. Start by seeing your worth so you can no longer be with people who don't.
192. No one can be everything to everyone.
193. I do not want to die remembering everything I did not get to do.
194. If it doesn't feel like the rest of the world loves you right now, that's okay. You need to love yourself right now.
195. You're not needy for having needs.
196. You don't need to be kind to be strong, but you need to be strong to be kind.
197. Crying over things you thought you already moved on from is okay, but let time do the heavy lifting for you.
198. Just because you're still learning to carry your burdens well does not mean they are too heavy for this world.
199. One day, you will see that something will bloom out of all you are doing. That something will be you.
200. It might not have ended the way you wanted it to, but it gave you the strength you didn't have.

201. When it feels like things are falling apart, it may just mean that things are falling into place.
202. You have not yet met all of the people who will fall in love with you. Why not start with getting to know yourself?
203. You deserve every emotion. Not just happiness, but sadness, anger, and everything in between.
204. The watered-down version of you will never let you grow.
205. The day you begin to accept yourself is the day you stop looking for acceptance from the world.
206. No one is worth sacrificing your mental health, including yourself.
207. Direction and speed are important: don't just be going nowhere fast.
208. The greatest middle finger you can give to a cruel world is when you give yourself more love than it can ever take from you.
209. Don't be impatient when waiting for what you deserve by settling for less.
210. Small habits define our largest traits.
211. You're going to figure it out just like you always have.
212. The energy you keep around you is the energy you let into you.
213. You're the hardest on yourself, and that's why you deserve a gold star.
214. Needing a day of rest does not set back your progress.
215. Nothing will break you as much as a vision you haven't fixed.
216. Another chapter can always come along and change your story.

217. You are the grown-up you did not think you would survive to be.
218. Being a good person means being good to yourself first.
219. Never feel guilty for saying no.
220. Unfortunately, we're still not robots and we still have hearts.
221. Trusting that everything will be okay is a choice.
222. Rejection can disguise redirection.
223. If you know you can do better, then the world will not stop you from doing better.
224. You need to move differently if you want results to look differently.
225. We were not made for everyone to like us.
226. Just because you are scared does not mean you cannot handle it.
227. Take the first step even if you don't see the last step yet.
228. Do it for the friends you have not met.
229. Making mistakes exposes faking perfection.
230. Worrying never did anything to change what comes.
231. The only person you can always convince to be on your side is you.
232. Time does not have a return policy; spend it with intention.
233. The same light you see in others is what others see in you.
234. Do it yourself. Do it *for* yourself.
235. You have so much to offer the person who will wake up in your body tomorrow.
236. It's okay to say, "Not today."
237. Prove them wrong.
238. The only way out of a tough situation is through it.

239. Your comfort zone is not always your safe zone. Know the difference.
240. You are meant to be everything you want to be and meant to be in every situation you are in.
241. The past is to be learned from, not lived in.
242. You can outgrow your trauma, pain, and the people that caused them.
243. You deserve things you think are too good to be true.
244. Evolve yourself. Don't just move forward.
245. Good memories make for poor covers of red flags.
246. Happiness is a choice we make for ourselves.
247. If you want to see the rainbow, you need to outlive the storm.
248. Behind every strong person is a story that gave them no choice but to be strong.
249. Autumn is beautiful when everything is dying. Let your past die beautifully as well.
250. Knowing your boundaries does not make you fragile. Be brave enough to know your breaking points.
251. Tolerance is addictive behavior.
252. Stop looking for light and become your light.
253. What you have survived did not kill you.
254. Doubts will kill you more than your fears will.
255. You don't owe loyalty to anyone in this world.
256. Do not let anyone with dirty feet walk through the garden of your mind.
257. Celebrate your small wins because only you understand what they took.
258. You are not your thoughts but the person who notices their existence in your head.
259. We do not become who we want by staying as we were.

260. Respect your own journey like you respect everyone else's.
261. Change is scary. Change is also good.
262. Do not ruin today by thinking about tomorrow.
263. No amount of anxiety will ever change your future. No amount of guilt will ever change your past.
264. Just because you want to be a better version of yourself does not mean you are not beautiful already.
265. Accept and honor where your feet are standing.
266. Know when you have the time and when to make the time you don't have.
267. It's not always about what you look at in the mirror, but what you see instead.
268. Growth is uncomfortable because you've never been there before. Do not fear growth.
269. If it feels like life has lost its magic, it might be time to learn a new trick.
270. Change is painful, but never as painful as staying in the same place you are stuck in.
271. At the end of every plateau is a cliff. Learn to fly before you reach that edge.
272. Healing has no instruction manual, no timeline, and no expectation.
273. Isn't it about time you gave yourself permission to stop surviving and start living?
274. To love who you are, you cannot hate the experiences that have brought you here.
275. Lose all interest in maintaining others' perceptions of you.
276. You've already survived 100 percent of your hardest days.

277. You are not your emotions, only the person who feels them.
278. You do not need to know why you are filled with hope just yet.
279. You are not meant for everyone, but you are meant for you.
280. Trees grow in silence.
281. We cannot expect change to happen overnight, but welcome it with open arms if it does.
282. If you weren't ready, be grateful that you kept yourself safe.
283. Happiness is not the absence of disappointment but the discovery of your strength through it.
284. How do you know that something better is not on its way?
285. Trauma does not shrink over time. Instead, we grow around it over time.
286. You are amazing, but amazing is not for everyone.
287. Waiting until you receive what you want means you will never stop waiting.
288. When the sun shines, it does not care when the moon will come.
289. You are not asking for too much, but you may be asking in the wrong places.
290. Keep taking care of yourself, especially when you are tired.
291. Walk away from the people who never made the effort for you to stay.
292. Happiness is a job done on the inside. Never let anyone else have that role or power in you.

293. There will never be a right time, but you can make it the best time.
294. Lose them if it means finding the self you lost.
295. The last time you felt this way, you got through it. You can do it again.
296. It will never be as big as it feels.
297. It is never your fault alone.
298. Things will always feel harder before they get better, so don't give up just yet.
299. You make the world a better place when you start to notice the flowers you leave behind.
300. You don't need a new you. You just need a healed you.
301. Don't forget to clear the clouds around your anxiety to find the hope underneath.
302. Pain and trauma do not belong to you. You can let go of them without losing a part of you.
303. Watering a dead plant will not bring it back to life. Water yourself when you need it.
304. We're all made of gold, so don't keep the people who only see rocks.
305. The chance to turn back was never there. Start seeing what is in front of you instead of what is behind.
306. Stop seeing the good in people if it means you cannot start seeing the good in yourself.
307. You need to stop touching a wound in order to let it heal.
308. Be impressed with your own effort.
309. Decide what kind of life you want and then learn to say no to anything else.
310. You're too young to believe that it will not be okay.
311. Thank the people who showed you what love is not.
312. If you were not the right person for you, it's okay to let go of that part of you.

313. Don't love the wrong people to avoid loving yourself.
314. You do not need to hurt someone to move on.
315. Teach your heart to accept what cannot be changed.
316. When you are stuck between a rock and a hard place, the only way out is up.
317. Reciprocate poor treatment with your absence.
318. Only you will ever know how far you have come, so yours is the only opinion that matters.
319. Whatever progress you make, do not let it go unnoticed even if you are the only one who will see it.
320. Learn how to choose your emotional reactions so you do not need to confront the consequences of self-destruction.
321. You'll regret being overly careful more than you'll regret taking chances.
322. Taking the time and enjoying the space between where you are and where you are heading is okay.
323. Listen to yourself first. Are you listening to what you are saying or are you just hearing?
324. You don't need to always be busy to be valuable.
325. What is the purpose of constantly worrying about the future if you cannot even live in the present?
326. Do what you need to do even if it means doing it alone.
327. If it is no longer in your hands, then it should no longer be in your thoughts.
328. You need to give up your weights if you want to learn to fly.
329. Letting yourself be alone in dark places is okay as long as you remember your way out.
330. Be the person you have been looking for.
331. Do not take criticism from someone you would not take advice from.

332. Our days are not measured by degrees of productivity but by degrees of presence.
333. Do not look back in anger or forward with fear, but look around with gratitude.
334. See the best in yourself like you wish others did.
335. The day you plant the seed is not the same day you will harvest the fruit.
336. Just because things could have been different does not mean that they could have been better.
337. Clouds can carry in a violent storm or be the color to a sunrise.
338. Your past is practice for where you are today.
339. Reveal who you have been scared of being.
340. Learn to move in silence, because you don't need an audience that does not see or hear you.
341. Share your pains with the people who want you to also share your joys.
342. Prioritize yourself enough to know how to remove yourself from the places where you do not feel safe.
343. Check in with yourself when no one else does.
344. Let what breaks your heart into two fix what you see.
345. Tell yourself what you don't want to hear, but also tell yourself what you need to hear.
346. The mornings when you wake up with a heavy heart will end.
347. Learn to accept apologies you may never receive.
348. When we are left in the cold, we learn to warm ourselves.
349. Understand yourself to love yourself.
350. You're growing and it's uncomfortable, but it's uncomfortable and you're growing.
351. One day, you will never have to say "one day" again.

352. Develop the thick skin to choose honesty over perfection every single time.
353. Be with people who will fit into your future instead of your history.
354. If it was not meant for you, then you are not missing out on anything.
355. Nobody can teach you your strength when your strength comes from inside of you.
356. Don't spend years searching for answers outside of yourself when they have always been inside.
357. I hope you go to sleep every night free of regret and revenge.
358. You don't need to discuss your healing with the world.
359. Feed your mind the way you feed your stomach.
360. Baggage does not stay with us forever.
361. Have you told the past version of you that everything will be more okay than they thought?
362. Strong people still need their hands held and reminders to hold their heads higher.
363. Don't stop until you're proud of who you have become.
364. The caterpillar does not know it will become a butterfly until it wakes up.
365. Get used to feeling happy. Get used to things working out.

PART III

GIVE YOUR HEART
THE SAFE SPACE
WITHIN THE
PRESENCE OF THE
PEOPLE WHO WILL
RESPECT YOUR
STORY AND
VULNERABILITIES

VULNERABLE

#37: Give your heart the safe space in the presence of people who will respect your story and vulnerability.

The bystander effect is such a rational, expected human response. At the same time, it is pitiful.

The bystander effect is when you are on the train and notice an elderly individual harassed for money by an aggressor. The train is packed in the middle of a Saturday afternoon, and you are not the only one whose eyes shift toward the commotion. The harassment continues for a few more painful minutes before the train skids to a stop, the aggressor runs off with a stuffed pocket of cash, and the elderly individual tries to recollect themselves. The tense air grows palpable: Why did no one step in?

When in crowds, we all expect someone else to step in. We look at those around us and come up with excuses about why we are not the chosen one to save the day, why someone else should be the savior. After all, just one person needs to step in, right? Even if it was not me, as long as someone helped the victim everything is all right.

The bystander effect is selfish. But it cannot be denied that the effect is our brain's strategy to protect us from reckless danger. What if we jumped in and the aggressor became violent? What if they had a hidden weapon and were not afraid to use it? Considering all these what-ifs, it seems a better idea not to intervene. The bystander effect tells us to leave that role to someone else. Let someone else do it. Someone else will, right?

"Let someone else be vulnerable because I cannot be that person."

I wonder what that says about human nature?

Unfortunately, we are all victims of the bystander effect. Our brains convince us we are not "someone else." Statistically speaking, that is impossible. If everyone has a someone else, then we are guaranteed to be the someone else in another narrative. However, we do not step up to be that someone as often, if ever. We do not step up to be vulnerable.

What does it mean when both the scariest and most courageous actions are the same?

I find it pitiful that we are always waiting for someone else. In society we see social trends develop and masses of people shifting from here to there simply because the momentum of those around them causes them to move too. We follow what seems to be popular among the crowds we identify with, and we unanimously share opinions because "everyone else does too." Denying the power of a society is impossible, and even more impossible is saying we are unaffected. It feels good to belong and fit in with groups we want to be with and the easiest way to keep up is to move with that group's direction.

However, even these directions are made by individuals in the group. Someone needed to be the first. Someone else needed to be vulnerable and shift the movement.

How scary is it to be someone else?

Our communities and societies, much like the humans making them up, revere strength, courage, and power. We naturally gravitate toward and want to be near characteristics we admire. However, humans are not built to always have strength, courage, and power. We were all helpless toddlers at one point and could not take a single step without falling over. No one gets to where they are without challenging experiences, but we idolize results over progress. If those around us are showing off their own strength and success, we become discouraged to speak up until we feel we have something to show. We become paralyzed to share anything but the parts society tells us it wants to see.

The bystander effect is more than a train ride on a Saturday afternoon. This phenomenon is a vicious cycle we have been running since we were born. Exceptions always apply to the majority's rule, and "someone else" makes these exceptions. The inability to recognize when we should be or already are that "someone else" is a handicap we are all burdened with.

The only exposure I had to mental health was a one-week course during my seventh-grade science class. We watched a short, impersonal video about the symptoms of mental disorders. We were instructed on identifying symptoms, who to talk to, and what steps can be taken to alleviate the symptoms. After the video was over, the classroom lights turned back on and that was the end of any mental health discussions. No one spoke about it the way we spoke about atoms or the states of matter, so in our developing minds mental disorders were the exception to the rules. We were taught how difficult they were to live with, but we also developed the idea that they were for "someone else." We were normal, part of "everyone else."

Lack of conversation around a topic is what makes it the exception to the common rule. Until a topic is normalized and spoken about regularly, space for the "someone else" idea will always exist in our heads. The separation of everyone else and someone else allows the continued existence of the bystander effect, making vulnerability rare among others while prevalent within ourselves.

It sounds ridiculous when I mention it now: I did not recognize my own symptoms of mental disorders. Even after the lovely video in my seventh-grade class, I did not point to myself and say, "Hey, I experience those too." Instead, I naturally fell into the same thoughts as my class: the symptoms I watched on the screen were for "someone else," not me. A seventh grader who cut herself at night was blinded and unable to recognize the same behavior as the cutting she saw in a full-screen educational video.

When I was first diagnosed with depression and anxiety, I had the same thoughts. Those words—"depression" and "anxiety"—never existed in my personal vocabulary. I read them in books and saw them in science videos, yet I never heard them used in conversations with others around me. I was in disbelief that they could apply to me. For so long, they were for the "someone elses" of this world. Mental disorders were for "someone else," not me. Never mind that I was regularly self-harming and considering suicide.

How scary it is to think about all we fail to recognize because we deem them unapplicable to ourselves.

All it takes is one "someone else" to propose a new direction. It takes just one step forward for others to see that, perhaps, what they were keeping inside is not as uncommon as they thought. When we live in societies prioritizing strength, courage, and power, there is no room for vulnerability anymore. Vulnerability is squeezed out of dialogues and conversations because it lacks the glamour of success stories. When we live in societies that do not encourage conversations about our uncertainties, our struggles, and our growth, how can we expect to recognize much less be okay with the very parts of us that make us human?

How can we believe we are not alone when we are raised to feel alone amid everyone else? When everyone else is showing off their good parts as they were raised to do, how can we believe there are others with unsorted loose ends?

None of us want to feel alone in this world, but none of us are able to be the first to show we do not want to be alone. Instead, we harbor these wishes within us, falsely leading ourselves to believe no one else shares what is truly a universal emotion. Why has it become so difficult to admit that each and every single one of us is human underneath the layers we choose to show the world?

Being human means having struggles, growth, progress, and learning. Being human is not a weakness, yet we let ourselves perpetuate a world that labels it a vulnerability. Since when did being human become a sign of weakness, a part of ourselves we are scared to show others?

Since when did we fear being human?

All it takes is one someone else to speak up for another someone else to join in, and then another, and then another, until these "someone elses" are no longer someone else, but everyone else.

We built up our walls because other humans showed us how to. Some of these walls are built from unfortunate experiences and protect us from dangers, but we were born with walls already built for us when we were born into a society discouraging vulnerability. We learned to build more walls when we saw everyone else building theirs. These walls stopped us from both seeing each other and being seen by others.

We are not single-handedly responsible for the walls we build around ourselves, but we are responsible for the walls we show others how to build. What does it take for us to start tearing down the walls between us so we can feel safe without them? Were our walls always this high and this many? Why is a world without walls so feared, idealistic, and unrealistic? Why is it that underneath all this human cynicism and pessimism we all wish we could have fewer walls and more connections?

Being vulnerable is one of the scariest things we can do, but being vulnerable is also one of the most courageous things we can leave behind. In the current day, being human means being vulnerable. However, we are only vulnerable when we feel that those around us can hurt us. We should be building together as humans, not as bodies afraid to make the first step toward connection. All it takes to show us the courage of vulnerability is someone else whose desire for the world to be a bit more human is stronger than their desire to protect themselves in an inhuman world.

Maybe we will take that first step at being someone else, bearing our vulnerabilities to the world. Maybe I will write a book and share raw and unfinished parts of myself, and maybe it will not be well received by everyone. But maybe it will reach the hands of one person who is also feeling alone. Maybe it can help that person feel a bit less alone so they, too, bear their vulnerabilities for others to see. Maybe that person will reach others who are feeling alone.

Maybe, one day, being human will no longer be a vulnerability but the connection we always shared. I can only hope so.

SEPTEMBER 2

11:12 p.m. Sometimes you use the phrase "what you're going through" when you talk about my experiences and my current state. I don't like it.

I know to everyone else it looks like I'm suffering a lot. It looks like I'm dealing with problems of sexual assault and depression and anxiety. Maybe you're right. Maybe I do go through a lot in my everyday life. But I'm not weak.

I know I crumble. I know I fall. I know I rely on my crutches at times. But I still get up.

To me, as someone who has been "going through a lot" since I can remember, this is simply everyday life. Sure, you can say it sounds empty or that it sounds like I'm jaded to what I'm experiencing. Maybe to you I am. But to me, this is my lifestyle. Sometimes I pause throughout my day, reflecting and looking back on some of the harder times I've had. Sometimes I am paralyzed during the day. Sometimes I break down. Sometimes I cry. And sometimes I don't. But I don't think I'm "going through" anything right now. If anything, I'm on a path of recovery.

I know it doesn't look like that to you, but it's what I feel. **And all I can ask is that you trust me and have faith that I am getting better.** I know I'm getting better. I know I'm growing stronger. I'm standing up again.

Please don't think I'm still suffering. Please don't make it sound like I'm "going through a lot" right now. To me, the worst is over. I'm simply dealing with the after waves. And I hope you don't discount my strength because of that.

SOME CHAPTERS DO NOT HAVE AN ENDING BECAUSE NOT KNOWING IS BETTER THAN CHASING AN ANSWER YOU DO NOT NEED

UNANSWERED QUESTIONS

#136: Some chapters do not have an ending because not knowing is better than chasing an answer you do not need.

"I know. I know what I'm feeling. But I'm just so tired. I . . . just don't want to try. I don't want to continue anymore."

"Then why are you still talking to me?"

The week had been particularly difficult for me with suicidal thoughts plaguing me at spontaneous instances. I was exhausted from existing. I found myself often asking why I still got out of bed every morning, why I still tried anymore.

I had a therapy session that afternoon to discuss and process what I was feeling. Although my therapist had worked with me for a while, I already had a sense of self-awareness and often knew how I was feeling and what I *should* do about it. My therapist's words were simply for affirmation and validation of those thoughts.

Our session started like many others before it. I detailed the events leading me to where I was, and together we walked through why my heart felt the way it did. As usual, he shared strategies and actions I could use to escape the feeling. Unlike usual, however, I interrupted him.

"I know. I know what I'm feeling. But I'm just so tired. I . . . just don't want to try. I don't want to continue anymore. I don't know why I'm still trying to fix myself."

He did not miss a beat. "Then why are you still talking to me?"

This is the question I have not been able to answer, even now. Did I not just mention I wanted to give up? Then what propelled me to email my therapist, schedule a call, and show up? Many similar questions were asked by friends and loved ones. "Why are you still living, then?" "Why do you still wake up in the morning?" I myself had posed these questions before, especially on those particularly hard days when I wanted nothing more but to shut the world out and exist in isolation.

I cannot tell you why I reached out to my therapist. The easy answer is I wanted to stop feeling the way I did. But does that not run contrary to my aforementioned feelings of wanting to give up trying to fix myself? I cannot tell you why I still wake up every morning, brush my teeth, put on fresh clothing, and get ready for my day when, in my head, desires to cease existing fill my thoughts.

I believe a small part of me wishes for my healing. Though it may be small, that part is strong enough to keep me reaching out and living. I may not be able to put the answer into words, yet the pursuit of this answer keeps me going. I want to know why I am still talking to my therapist and why I am still living. It's okay that I don't have the answer yet.

I think the unanswered questions say the most.

JULY 9

8:27 a.m. I have a meeting in three minutes. It's been nice to dedicate some time to this journal and my thoughts in the morning, and to show myself that it's beneficial to dedicate time to this. If my mind is calm later, I would like to start expanding on the thoughts I've been having for the past week, focusing less on the conversations I've been having during the day and more on the thoughts I need to address. But I won't be able to make that step until my mind feels ready and safe to do so. I cannot force myself to reach that point even though I want to, so I am also learning to respect my own speed and progress. Let's see how things turn out today. I've found that every day changes every hour, and my mind jumps all over the place.

3:53 p.m. Work call is over now. **Sometimes I cannot help but ask why life has been so unfair to me. Am I currently paying for something incredibly heinous that I'm going to do in the future?**

At the same time, I feel incredibly numbed to everything going on. It's like I don't feel any worse. I'm just here. Maybe this is better than being sadder, but I think it may mean I haven't been hit yet. I'm scared. I'm going to be hit soon.

4:10 p.m. I nap for two hours, but when I wake up I feel like I overslept. It makes me feel sick and makes my head hurt. I can't even sleep and I'm sleep-deprived. I want to die. I'm not even suicidal. I just don't have motivation to do anything. I want to just waste away.

YOU CAN NOT FLIP
THE NEXT PAGE
OF YOUR STORY IF
YOU ARE STUCK
REREADING THE
LAST ONE

IDENTIFIED PROBLEMS

#162: You cannot flip the next page of your story if you are stuck rereading the last one.

Every good story begins with an introduction, courses through a conflict, and wraps up with a resolution. The princess is trapped in a tower with a dragon, and a knight in shining armor swoops in to save the day. They live happily ever after. The end.

The story would be quite the uneventful quest if the dragon was left out. Our characters would have no chance to develop, as they would have no reason not to continue on with their undisturbed, merry lives. The story truly begins when the dragon is introduced. In our own stories, as our own narrators, we need to identify those dragons, those problems we try to solve.

Before you can even hope to see change in your life, you need to know what you are changing. You need to identify which problems in your life are so instrumental to who you are that fixing them could mean a lifetime of positive change. The problem with that, however, is that we all have problems with identifying our problems.

If only our lives were like the math problems we did in kindergarten, where apples and lima beans modeled equations. These problems were solved by taking away or by adding. Sometimes, if the problems were more complicated, then addition developed into multiplication or subtraction into division. Such problems were so simple, so logical, and so easily made sense. If Jill had five apples and gave Sam three, then she had two left. No ifs, ands, or buts complicated the problem solving. Even as we grew older and took more complicated math classes, math never changed from its calculated and logical nature. An equal symbol always connected the left and right sides of the equation. All we needed to do was piece together its elements and we could balance both ends.

Unfortunately, our lives cannot be modeled by simple math equations. Our problems are not defined for us in neat mathematical terms. We wish for that floating equal sign always guaranteeing some form of balance. If only we knew what we needed to add, subtract, multiply, or divide to maintain the balance in our lives. If only it were easy. Instead, our lives are defined as problems missing their pieces. We may know which results we want to see on the right-hand side of the equation, but we do not know what to piece together in order to get there. Sometimes, both sides are complex equations, and we are caught trying to understand how they could possibly work together.

Step back for a moment.

Do we truly know what is on the other side of the equal sign? Do we truly know what goal we are working toward?

"It's like I know what's on the right side of the equal sign, yet I have all these loose pieces on the left. I don't know what expressions can even be used on what. How do I even begin to sort out this mess to reach my right-side goal?"

Take a moment to ask yourself why you do what you do. Why do you work so hard in your life? Why do you talk to the people you talk to, or live in the place where you live? Why do you not do the things you do not do? Are the answers to these questions what you want to put on the right side of your equation?

The right side of the equation, the conventional "result" of a mathematical equation, can be used as starting points for understanding the workings of the left. By working backward, we are able to use the end goal to reach our first steps. Therefore, properly defining the right side of your equation is absolutely necessary, especially for goals of self-development.

Whatever this right side of the equation may be for you, realize that you can and should frame it as a problem's solution. You need the perspective that this goal is meant to "fix" something in your life which you do not currently feel fulfilled by. Someone who may have the right-side goal of loving their body more can see their present problem is a lack of self-confidence. Someone with the right-side goal of ending a loop of abusive relationships can see their present problem is the inability to maintain healthy, lifelong relationships. This, my friend, is identifying the problem. Your right-side goal is the ideal solution you believe will fix this problem.

Sometimes we can dive deep into why such problems exist. Why do you lack self-confidence? Is it because you lack appreciation for yourself? Do you have a difficult time listening and believing the compliments of others? Do you compare yourself to others a bit more frequently than is healthy? You have the space to dig deep. Explore yourself. Explore your problems, why they exist, and where they come from.

We attack weeds at their root, not at their leaves.

Deciding which of your problems to focus on now versus later will be a recurring thought. Do not spend your life working on a right-side goal not rooted in a problem that deeply affects you. Accomplishing your goal will only happen when you acknowledge problems and work on them.

Defining what our problems are is not always easy. We do not have a beautiful mathematical equation laid out for us. In fact, these undefined problems are the very ones that lay the path for what we should be working on. If it proves easy for us to identify our own problems, then are they truly problems deserving of our devoted time and energy? If your problems are low-hanging and easily visible and if you have yet to fix them, then the problem you should be addressing is a completely separate problem. The problems you often fail to recognize are those most deeply rooted in you and can only be noticed when self-reflection and introspection lead you to face yourself.

So why do we care so much about defining the problem? Why not just jump straight into the action of fixing ourselves and working on who we want to become? Is this all a waste of time—attempting to define such hazy and vague problems—when instead we could be enacting our next steps? We need to define our problems first because acknowledgment of their existence is the first step to healing.

I like to say the first step of healing is always the hardest, since this first step is simply being aware that you have a problem. Some of us refuse to face our problems so fiercely that our subconscious creates the illusion that we do not have any. In a way, our subconscious has forced us into ignorance. We all know people we simply do not understand. No matter how many times we tell them about their bad habit, they gape in genuine disbelief. To them, a world in which they have such imperfection simply does not exist. Sure, they may have other flaws, but not this one. They have created their own illusion of its inexistence. We may dislike these people but find ourselves in similar scenarios through various interactions. To someone else, you may be that person with incredible ignorance of how you wreak havoc on those around you. Your subconscious has already created a world where you and this problem simply do not coexist, so it would seem impossible to you. Ignorance is bliss, they say.

Unfortunately, working on the wrong problems is easy when we do not first define what exactly needs to be changed. We might spend months or years dedicated to solving something that turns out to be a surface-level symptom of a deep-seated problem. For some of us, we may realize this soon enough and backtrack so we are on course to solving our problems. Others may never realize it, living the next chapter of their lives with the original problem still unchanged. They may believe any efforts to change actually give rise to new problems and end up feeling defeated. Stay away from this kind of discouragement and stay on track with what you need to solve in yourself by first defining problem statements. After all, you cannot have any idea of where you are going if you do not first know where you have been.

Framing our problems for what they are is also a difficult step. Stay away from "I wish" statements, such as "I wish my job paid me more." This wording is not framing your problem as a problem but instead as a desire. All desires come from a place of inadequacy, where a need is not being met. That need is the problem. Make sure your problem statements reflect problems, not wishes.

Draw out the core from each of the problems on your list. This is my favorite part. You know how when you were in elementary school (or sometimes, for the unfortunate, even in middle school) there was always a student in your class who felt the dying need to incessantly ask your teacher, "But why?" Play that role. Distill your many problems down to a handful of patterns most common in your life.

Start by asking each of your problems two questions: Why is this problematic to me? Why is it not fixed yet? For example, if your first problem is that you feel your job does not pay you enough for your effort, then you can answer the questions like so:

- Why is this problematic to me? I do not feel valued enough in my workplace and I do not have enough money.
- Why is it not fixed yet? This is my third month at the job, and it does not feel appropriate yet to ask about promotions.

Continue doing this exercise until you start to notice trends between your problem statements. When you look at all your problem statements, derived from constantly asking the same two questions from your original problems, you should begin to see similar patterns come up. Some of these may reflect a lack of self-confidence, an inability to accept criticism, a fear of disapproval, and so on.

When do you stop asking these questions? The truth is that you should never stop asking yourself why issues are problematic for you or why they are not solved yet. Rather than dwelling on and remaining frustrated over the existence of these problems, explore what underlying causes exist. The problems you scribbled down in the initial stages are merely symptoms of the greater patterns at the core of your life. They are the small branches that result from applying your root problems to various parts of your life.

You don't get a "happily ever after" until your story is over. There may always be more dragons lurking around the corners, but you already won half the battles by having the courage to look the beasts in its eyes.

JULY 9
ROOTS
6:03 p.m. I mentioned that I did not exactly grow up with a lot of love, and my therapist stopped me and asked why I said that. He said the truth was that I never grew up with love and even the subtleties in my statement showed how I discounted my experiences. I still find it impossible to believe what my therapist said. I still hold it against myself, still doubt whether I truly am as deeply affected as he claims I am. How do I know I'm not just incredibly weak for allowing these problems to plague me for so long? I guess a part of getting better means being able to accept what everyone tells me about myself.

8:11 p.m. I needed to explain again today the basics of how my mental disorders affect me every day. If you are someone I have previously not explained this to, I apologize for how delayed this is and I hope this can help you.

AUGUST 10
TIME
It makes sense that I need time to make a full recovery, but I don't want to take time anymore. I've had my disorders for as long as I can remember. They have become a part of my growing up and development. I don't want to let them keep being a part of my life.

That's why I'm having these hard conversations with people. This is why I have therapy. There's so much unrooting to be done and I'm driven to make it happen.

MOTIVATION

I'm perfectly content with where I am without recovery. I've lived for so many years of my life without recovery. I don't constantly think about the fact I have depression every day. It's become a part of my every day and it's obvious in my thought processes and actions. It's the duality I struggle with. A part of me knows everyone else is telling me to get better, so I don't personally see a reason to get better other than because everyone else is telling me it's what I need. I want to be able to find that motivation in me *to get better.*

POV

I know it's hard for everyone to understand what my thought process is. I know others see my reality as "Emily deals with depression," but the way I see it I don't have any condition. Rather, this is my reality and how I grew up. While everyone thinks, "We want Emily to get better," the way I see it is, "Everyone wants me to change everything I've ever learned and developed in myself growing up." And that's why it's hard. That's why it's so deeply rooted in me and that's why it's so hard for everyone else to see the way I see or think the way I think. This is no one's fault. We just have different pairs of eyes. Depression is not a disorder to me the way others may categorize it. To me, it's my entire growing-up experience. This is not as simple as recovering from depression. For me, I need to change so much of my development.

Furthermore, as someone incredibly self-aware of my situation, so much of treatment does not work for me. Finding new insight with therapy is hard because I've been in my head for so long. I've already had the same conversations over and over again.

HIGH-FUNCTIONING DEPRESSION

My depression is called high-functioning depression, which means I'm usually the last person most people would expect to be depressed. I perform well as a high-achieving human who enjoys laughing and smiling and having fun with my friends, so much so most people often do not expect that I am struggling inside. However, when I am tested, I fall very quickly. It takes a lot for someone who is high functioning to fall, so when we do fall, we fall very deeply to a very bad headspace. I have medically diagnosed triggers. They are violence, loud noises in enclosed spaces, anger in enclosed spaces, forcing me to eat, and my brother. These are guaranteed triggers, but there are many other things that can trigger me depending on the context. I generally can conduct myself well to control my anxiety when I am triggered around people, but my eyes tell it all.

DISASSOCIATION

My strongest defense mechanism is my ability to disassociate at will. For most, disassociation is a defense mechanism that kicks in subconsciously to shut down and emotionally numb oneself. However, because I have done so quite frequently, I now have the ability to do so on command. I think it says a lot that I am able to disassociate myself consciously as a defense mechanism that should never have been readily available. I think it says a lot about how accustomed I am to hard realities. I think it says a lot.

READING

As an introvert having grown up how and where I did, I have always been very observant of the people around me. I pride myself in being able to read between the lines and understand the room's mood when I walk in. I spent most of my life being a passive human and have always observed people in the way they talk and carry themselves. That's why I tend to be quite fluent in reading the room or reading body language. When I meet people for the first time, I tend to also be able to tell how similar our experiences are. It's hard to explain how, but it really is in the small mannerisms—the things they say and choose not to say. I'm able to tell if they have had similar conversations. Maybe I'm wrong, but I don't tend to be.

8:35 p.m. Despite all of these, please know I am working harder than ever on my recovery. Only because I am facing my recovery am I able to be honest about who I am.

SLOW HEALING
DESERVES YOUR
CELEBRATION TOO

HEALING

#70: Slow healing deserves your celebration too.

"Are we there yet?" I asked for the thirteenth time. Our GPS said we were only a fraction of the way there, but our six-hour drive already felt twenty-four hours long. How come on long trips the road there feels longer than the way back?

Unlike long road trips, however, we do not get a GPS for healing. We do not even have maps. We do not have a road back, just a one-way ticket forward to places we may not even know yet. We get no estimated time of arrival or road signs showing us the right path.

Healing and change do not happen overnight. Sometimes they can, but, more often than not, attempts to unlearn what has already been ingrained within us will take more time than we anticipate. Sometimes this unlearning takes months. Sometimes it takes lifetimes, and we still feel like we are not "there" yet.

The hardest place I have been is being unable to recognize my own healing. All I could see was how far I was from the finish line. What made this even harder was not knowing if there was a finish line at all.

Seeing where you've already walked is always easier. While taking the first step is monumental for your own progress and healing, the steps following are equally difficult. Once you identify what your problems are and confirm that they need fixing, it only gets harder from there.

The road to healing is lined with traps we lay for ourselves. Just because we understand what needs to change does not mean we know the best way to change it—or whether we know how to change it at all. Even if we do understand how to change our situation, we are not always well-equipped to do so, or at least not as quickly as we would like. How easy it would be if we simply knew all the answers the instant we figured out which questions to ask!

I have been diagnosed with mental disorders for over ten years now, and I still have mornings when my first thought after waking up is, "Why do I still struggle with these same thoughts?" As I get dressed, I find ways to ridicule myself for not working on myself hard enough, for not being strong enough to support myself, and for not being at the place I want to be. Sometimes I remember how the Emily from a year ago promised herself she would be in a better place this year, and I cannot help but feel a heavy sense of disappointment that I was unable to uphold the promise.

On the train ride to work, I continue to think about my healing. I have been through a handful of therapists and attend regular sessions. I read literature on healing. I was once excited and motivated to make changes in my life. Why am I not there? Why have I not met all of the goals I set for myself? Last year's Emily was excited for this year's Emily to figure herself out more, but can I really say with confidence to last year's Emily that this Emily feels any more understood?

Unfortunately, these traps are set by our own impatient expectations for ourselves. We are harder on ourselves than we are on those around us. Is it not time you treat yourself with the same patience you have for those around you?

The traps are difficult to recognize. We beat ourselves up for not healing fast enough and tell ourselves our pace is because we are lazy, slow, and making excuses, so we bear sole responsibility for our inactivity. We trap ourselves into believing the expectations we set and then belittle ourselves when they cannot be met.

Humans seem to enjoy putting themselves through these vicious cycles, don't they?

We tell ourselves we should have been able to do things differently. We should be able to do things faster. We should be able to do things better. Nonetheless, we did not, and it is our fault. We could have used our time better. We could have been more careful in our steps. We could have thought into the future more. But we did not, and it is our fault.

We were blissfully ignorant of problems that needed fixing before, but now they have our attention and cannot leave our minds. Not only do we need to heal, we also have a voice in the back of our heads judging how we do it. This voice observes us with a careful eye, calling us out and criticizing us for every mistake.

That voice keeps us accountable for our progress. We should be grateful for it, yet it often becomes a voice we dread. It tells us our healing is not good enough.

The grass is always greener on the other side because when we stand in one spot we never get to see the grass underneath our feet. We see everyone else's progress while beating ourselves up for our own. Is it not time we gave ourselves the grace and the validation we deserve?

When I look back on my healing journey, I want to be proud of how far I have come. Progress may not always be linear, and it may have its relapses, but all that matters is that it trends upward and forward. Even the smallest bits of progress should be celebrated, not criticized. When we already did our best and are already pushing ourselves as hard as we can to become better versions of ourselves, there should only be encouragement coming from supporters, including ourselves. There should be no room for criticism when you have already gone through so much in your life and chosen to continue working on yourself instead of giving up.

You could have shrugged and walked away when you saw a difficult part of yourself. You could have let yourself continue living the way you were comfortable with. You could have stepped away. However, you chose to go through one more difficult challenge, one more uncomfortable change, and one more step forward. When we deserve to be proud of ourselves there is no room for criticism.

At the end of the day, the only opinion that matters is ours. We are the only people in the world we ever need to prove ourselves to. We are the ones stuck with ourselves for the rest of our lives, so it is time we begin getting along with ourselves.

Telling ourselves that we are doing a good job is not always easy. We strive for first-place trophies instead of participation medals, but when the participation medal requires your hardest effort, you are already a champion for trying your best. After all, we cannot ask for gold stars or perfection from ourselves in everything: all we can ask is that we do our best with the resources and information we have—and that's pretty great to me.

We may not have road maps to take us away from the traps laid on our paths, yet with time it gets easier and easier to spot them along the way. We just need to maintain faith that as long as we keep working on ourselves and keep pushing forward, we will get there one day.

JULY 27
9:34 a.m. I feel like I should still be broken. But it's up to me to allow myself to still be broken. It's okay if I feel this way. I can't change my thought process and self-love instantly. I just need to know I'm not going to let go of the progress I've made for anyone, including you. I'm sorry. But I need to do this for myself.

TURNING POINTS
The most hopeful thing he said to me today was something about myself that I had not realized before. I hadn't even told him about sophomore year of high school, which I see as the point when I hit rock bottom, yet he asked me, "How have you survived?" He went on, saying he was amazed how I've not only survived all these experiences but have had the will to continue fighting. He asked how I was able to continue seeking trust in others even though I know I'm not doing it properly. He asked how I was able to try to trust people anymore and how I was able to reach a point at which I could have physical contact again. He said I've been putting up such a fight for so long, he was amazed I'm still fighting through everything I've been dealing with.

I guess I just never looked at myself like that. I've never acknowledged or given credit to myself for how much I've been doing to fight. I kept looking at my losses, my mistakes, and the backward steps I've faulted. ***I blamed myself when I fall down but never gave myself the chance to realize that to fall down I had to have reached higher heights first.***

He told me I had so much power in me, so much drive and determination, that I've been fighting for so long and never, never gave myself that acknowledgment.

I think that cracked me.

His validation and recognition cracked me. **I never gave myself validation.** *I always brushed the thought aside, seeing myself as weak for the steps backward and beating myself up for never having the ability to be stable. I'm sorry to all of you who have been telling me the same, who have been trying to make me see this as well. That's the problem with this disorder: I hear everything but am selective with what goes through. I'm sorry to all of you who have been trying so hard to help me, but I was unable to accept it.*

Is it okay for me to accept my difficulties and, even more so, accept how hard I have been fighting?

1:38 p.m. Question: ***Does recovery ever end? Is there ever an end for someone like me, whose life will inarguably still be plagued every now and then?*** *As of now, I cannot believe I will ever be able to completely put these issues behind me and move forward the way I have before. But is this simply because I'm so far from the surface of the water I don't know it exists? Or does it truly not exist?*

2:16 p.m. I can't help but remember where I was one month ago, how you told me it would not be possible to change that much within a month. I know it's been a few days more since a month after that day, but even I would not be able to believe the amount of change I've been able to undergo. I'm a completely different person from who I was a month ago. Absolutely different. And it's amazing.

TAKE THE TIME
YOU NEED TO
HEAL YOUR INNER
CHILD

CHILDHOOD

#68: Take the time you need to heal your inner child.

One of the hardest truths for me to accept is that I am a product of how I was raised. I've been quite independent since middle school, working and taking care of myself because I did not want my family's interference. Due to constant disagreement and trauma, I did all I could to be as distant from them as possible. I even considered legal emancipation at sixteen, when a child can willingly "disown" themselves from their family.

I grew up wanting to be as different from them as possible. I did not want to carry any more of their imprints on me. I wanted to be completely removed from them, to be related in as minimal a degree as possible. Therefore, I took on too many responsibilities. I faulted myself when my bad habits arose, and I blamed myself for my anxieties. I became accustomed to regular self-deprecation. My aversion to any connection with my family had not allowed me to fathom that perhaps much of why I am the way I am is because of an undeniable legacy they left in me.

Regardless of whether or not we have an easy time admitting it, our parents leave deeply rooted mental and emotional impacts on us. Even if we do not pay attention to them, these legacies grow with us and can be more or less obvious in our behaviors.

In healthy families, these are legacies of love, respect, and healthy independence. In other families, these are legacies of fear, guilt, and self-deprecation. When families act in abusive manners toward children, similarly toxic behaviors become present in later stages of the child's life.

To be clear, in my opinion no family is toxic in nature. All parents and all families make their own mistakes. All families have their own problems and an inability to resolve them can lead to prolonged struggles. None of us are perfect. However, even parents who carry love for a child can still mistreat them. Most parents acting with toxic and abusive behaviors still say they love their children, and they really, truly mean it. However, parental love is more than simply expressing affection. Parental love is also a behavior. Therefore, there are no toxic families but families with toxic behaviors instead.

From my experience, repetitive, constant abusive behavior toward children could develop into an unhealthy upbringing and long-lasting emotional damage. Unfortunately, we often do not recognize these effects until it is too late.

As children, we are still molding together our ideas of what is good and bad. We have less ability to identify when our parents are exhibiting toxic behaviors versus disciplining behaviors. Frequently, when we are not given the opportunity to observe and reflect on how our upbringing effects our behaviors, we end up modeling the same behaviors in our parenting styles. After all, we only have one set of parents, and their modeling is the only form of teaching we have for parenting.

From my experience, this is intergenerational trauma: being unable to break out of a toxic cycle of unhealthy parenting styles because of abusive childhoods and exposure to toxic behaviors. Parents genuinely believe they are doing what is best for their children when they model their parenting styles after that of their parents, but such good intentions do not always carry parallel good consequences. Toxic parenting styles do not result in nourishing behaviors but in unloving behaviors wrapped with the thin label of love.

No wonder the children of abusive behaviors struggle with understanding what love is and further struggle to be parents capable of loving behaviors.

One of my greatest life goals is to break my intergenerational trauma. It feels nearly impossible at times to ask myself to objectively view my upbringing and reflect on whether the behavior I received as a child was loving or not. Discerning between abusive behavior and "behavior I deserved because of my disobedience" is difficult, especially when I know I tend to be more inclined to blame myself.

Intergenerational trauma is a vicious cycle growing stronger with each generation, but it is a cycle worth trying to break.

By working with my therapist, reading literature, reflecting on my behavior, and chatting with children of other households, I have collected data points for my own analyses. The more I learn, the more I find myself questioning my upbringing. This is not a comfortable process. Telling ourselves we grew up in a household of toxic family behaviors is never easy. I keep telling myself it will be worth it when I can promise my future generations a healthier family system.

Every family is a carefully designed system in which each person is connected with the next. We are affected by each other in profound and unspoken manners. We are a complicated network of human emotions dependent on needs, rules, and values. Yet, because these are unspoken, invisible systems, they are difficult to identify. In healthy families, these unspoken rules and systems are developed with the goal of what is best for all the family members. They are supportive and respectful to children's development. However, rules are not meant to be fixed in stone. We never truly know what is best for a growing child, as they are regularly developing and changing. The rules should reflect these variations.

It makes sense to begin with a loose set of unspoken rules to begin developing the family system instead. The loose makeup can be developed from the parents' best guesses of what is most supportive for the family, but even those are largely self-centered and self-serving when parents have no other reference points for what is best for the child. As long as rules are flexible and change as children develop, then the starting basis can be negligible. Yet when parents are unwilling to be flexible and change the unspoken rules according to the children's growth, they crystallize into what they always were—self-centered and self-serving.

Many unspoken rules have underlying toxic beliefs with a distorted perception of reality. Like in my family system, this creates environments where children are more prone to abuse. Because these unspoken rules are the values around which the rest of the family system is developed, children are vulnerable as they continue developing ideas about the world and themselves. Not wanting to disobey the family system and dependent on it for their safety, children are susceptible to blindly obeying family rules built on abusive behaviors without understanding how unfavorable their positions are.

Examples of unspoken toxic rules with underlying abusive behaviors from my upbringing are:
- Children need to respect their parents and what they say, no matter what. → Children cannot think they know more than their parents.

- Children should be seen but not heard. → Children cannot lead their own lives or make their own decisions.
- Children should spend as much time as possible in the house. → Children should always need their family and put them first above all.

A family system with no personal freedom for its members is a toxic system. What distinguishes a healthy family system from my unhealthy family system is freedom and liberties among its members. I notice healthy families encourage freedom in their children through a gradual but sure release on parental control. When children are toddlers, they are completely under the care of their guardians to keep them safe and make decisions for them. However, it does not make sense for a fully grown adult to still be under their parents' care to the level of when they were a toddler. The eventual and slow release of control from the parents is what helps the fully grown adult make their own responsible decisions. With the release of control comes the introduction of freedom and autonomy to express oneself as the individual they are. Children should be encouraged to develop their own individuality, responsibility, and self-worth, none of which can be developed if they are never given the chance to explore the world on their own.

In my family system, individual expression was discouraged, and everyone conformed to the value system of the parents. Personal boundaries were blurred when I received the message that I could not be an individual separate from the family unit. I no longer had a sense of self and was treated as an extension of the family system. Environments become suffocating when a child's ill-advised efforts to gain their own sense of control are perceived as disobedience and result in a tightening of rules.

These kinds of unhealthy environments reinforce ideas in children that promote dependency. In some cases, children need constant approval from their parents to make any decisions even when making the smallest choices. Such dependency dictates the rest of the child's development, confirming the urgency to cut intergenerational traumas. This kind of unhealthy dependency affected me in later developmental stages when I was unable to make decisions and needed validation or approval from others instead of myself. However, the most unfortunate result of abusive behaviors in my childhood was my inability to realize they were abusive behaviors.

It became a lifestyle for me to deny my parents' toxic actions. Many people might have trouble understanding how their relationship with their guardians deeply impacts the rest of their life. Children grow up with their families as their main frame of reference for how they develop their lives, and the toxic teachings they grow up with become permanently carved as truths.

Identifying abusive behaviors is difficult when we are the victims of them. We do not see abuse when that is all we know. Furthermore, families with toxic behaviors, like mine, tend to be professionals at showing a very normal facade to the rest of the world. To everyone else, our family unit looked like any other. The more normal our family acted in public, however, the more toxicity was hidden in private. Parents with toxic behaviors tend to already possess narcissistic tendencies, causing them to believe they are better parents than they truly are. After all, a parent with abusive behavior acts out of what they think is best for their family or what they think is loving behavior, oblivious to the self-serving nature and consequences they blind themselves from. When my parents and I live in denial, recognition has less room to emerge.

While I've listed common toxic behaviors I've experienced below, this list is nowhere near exhaustive. Toxic parental behaviors are built on judgment, criticism, and inflexible rules leading to low self-esteem, and may look like any of the following:

- Calling children names or insulting them in public/in front of others
- Constantly criticizing children under the guise of "pushing them harder"
- Misusing substances or alcohol in the presence of children
- Inflicting physical pain as punishment
- Becoming emotionally unavailable when children are in need of support
- Forcing children into positions of taking care of the parents or feeling responsible for the parents' emotions
- Making children fear the parents as a means to achieve obedience
- Shutting down any expression of anger or dissatisfaction from children toward the parents by claiming the children are ungrateful
- Accusing children of actions without first listening to their stories

Any of the above behaviors can lead children to a lifelong struggle of ruined self-esteem and damaged relationships. Because my parents were my first interaction and representation of love, our toxic relationship disabled my ability to develop healthy relationships into adulthood. This manifests in me through damaged worldviews and behaviors including abusive romantic relationships, the inability to believe people will not abandon me, an expectation of the worst in people, a fear of showing myself honestly to others, a distanced understanding of myself, a paralyzing need for perfection, and the unstable inability to rest.

Ouch.

It makes sense that all healthy relationships, whether between parents and children or between friends and lovers, require vulnerability and trust from all parties. Toxic families remove the children's belief that this can be possible. To them, the world is already dark before they get to explore it.

No standard type of toxic behavior exists in parents and family units. Damage is likely sourced from generations back, when parents themselves were submitted to toxic behaviors in their upbringing. Pointing to when intergenerational traumas were first introduced is nearly impossible, but it can be identified when they are perpetuated. Step back and see the urgency in finding how to stop such cycles.

It also makes sense that all children, like everyone else, have their needs to survive. They have their physiological needs of food, clothing, and shelter, but they also have needs for healthy mental development. Children need emotional nurturing and respect for their feelings, as well as the right to make mistakes and be disciplined without crossing into abuse. They have the right to be children and to spend their childhood years being playful and silly. Without this phase, they are unable to learn how to exercise responsibility or how to make trade-off decisions between irrationality and consequences.

Children in abusive households similar to mine are forced to grow up too quickly and are robbed of their right to being children. My parents, like many other parents with abusive behaviors, were unable to honor my ability to be a child. I grew up watching friends enjoy their time as children while I was forced to act like an adult without guidance. And because I was unable to fulfill adult responsibilities as well as adults (who are actually meant to carry those responsibilities), I began a lifetime walk of feeling inadequate and inferior.

Instead of nourishing their children with household duties teaching responsibility, toxic parents enforce requirements at the sacrifice of their childhoods. Like me, these children take on their parents' impossible standards as their own and develop expectations for themselves that lead to workaholism and perfectionism. As children, they look for constant validation from their parents, but because such is unattainable they carry the need for external affirmation into their adulthoods.

And how can we expect such children to develop self-worth if they do not even have the opportunity to develop themselves?

When parents compare their children to others or use constant criticism as supposed encouragement, expecting the child to feel good about who they are is impossible. I lost my ability to create an identity for myself when I was humiliated for my development. It felt like nothing I did could ever be good enough and there would always be something wrong with me. Furthermore, when a parent failed to protect me from the other parent's criticism, it was communicated that their words were tolerable, acceptable, and, worst of all, true.

Children in these situations develop anxious personalities, living in fear of comparison because of regular manipulation in their youth. Every form of manipulation, whether in childhood or adulthood, forces them into a corner where only two survival options are available: either give in and stay safe from attack, or rebel. As a child, the first option looked like the only option when my worldview was limited to what existed in our family. However, we all heard stories of children who rebelled and became complete opposites of all they were raised to be.

Can you really blame them when they felt suffocated for so long? I cannot when I see rebellion reflected so deeply within myself.

In my humble opinion, strong reactions to interactions with our parents are an obvious symptom of the emotional scars they left on us. Children growing up with parents of toxic behaviors are left with emotional legacies that stop them from living the life they desire. As long as those legacies of hurt exist within us, we struggle with being ourselves. This is hard to identify at times. For some, it looks like the continued need to submit and prioritize their parents' approval, and for others like myself, it looks like rebellion and alienation at any cost.

If intergenerational trauma is already engraved in us, do we stand a chance at changing what generations before us could not?

Unlearning our childhood isn't easy. We admittedly would not be who we are today if we had not gone through what we did, but we also carry hurt that is reflected in unhealthy habits we still drag behind us. If we continue to drag those unhealthy habits into our future relationships, we become responsible for perpetuating intergenerational traumas.

As children from abusive households, we can take steps to alleviate their effects on us. Identifying and recognizing the abuse in our childhood is the first step forward, yet what follows is often more difficult to learn.

We can change ourselves without changing our parents. I reached a comforting acceptance of the fact that my parents are also products of intergenerational trauma. I am in control of my life as much as they are in control of theirs. For years, I desperately attempted to show them my hurt and trauma, but their own beliefs in their parenting behaviors kept them from hearing me. They already ran the course of being parents. Therefore, I cannot be the one to change them anymore. I must focus my efforts toward myself. This is not defeat but the liberty to let go of what I cannot change.

I do not know who needs to hear this, but I know I needed to: we can overcome our childhood trauma, hurt, and abuse even without our families changing. We do not need our abusers' permissions to heal.

We do not need to forgive our abusers to heal. The desire for revenge might just be the weight preventing us from moving on. Similarly, forcing ourselves to forgive our abusers may be a fantasy stopping us from seeing reality. Forgiveness is not forgiveness if it is simply a disguise to pretend the abuse didn't happen; that is called forgetting.

While it is possible to forgive our abusers, it can only help us when forgiveness is reached at the end of the process, not the start. Forgiveness is never the first step to healing. We need to give ourselves the time and space to grieve, reflect, and process the hurt we were put through. We need to reconcile with the fact that we did not receive the love from our families we were promised. We need to step out of denial and stop discounting the damage we were engraved with. Pretending to not see its existence is just about as good as hiding an elephant under a rug and passing by it every day—just like how we will be hiding the hurt in our heart underneath an act of forgiveness.

Forgiveness might be appropriate if abusers recognize and acknowledge their actions, take responsibility, and have a mature conversation with their victims about what steps forward can look like. However, that does not happen very often.

And that's okay.

As a child raised in toxic parenting, I found that emotional peace comes for children raised by toxic parents when we are able to release ourselves from the hold of the emotional legacies controlling us. This means recognizing our families' toxic behaviors are reflections of them, not us. It means letting go of our sense of responsibility and learning we are not responsible for their toxic behaviors toward us. Even if malicious intent was not driving their actions, the results and scars remain.

It means identifying our grief and pain without attempting to suppress them, as grieving is an active process of healing rather than a passive one.

It means learning to have emotional expression in reaction to the abusive behaviors of our families. Anger is not a privilege but an emotion all humans share. Learn to healthily deal with anger you may have kept simmering on the back burner.

It means breaking abusive and unhealthy relationship patterns with your family. Wanting to take care of yourself is not selfish.

It means growing into an adult in your family unit. Being an adult means you have responsibilities you may not have learned in an abused childhood: responsibilities to be your own individual, to honestly review your childhood, to acknowledge painful connections between your families' behaviors and your own, to lessen their power and impact in your adult life, to call yourself out and pause when you notice similarly abusive behavior toward yourself and others, and to seek resources and support to heal your inner abused child.

It means being okay with who you are and being okay with your family being who they are. Emotional independence does not mean separation. You can be part of your family while being an individual. Standing up for yourself does not mean you are cutting off connections.

Lifelong endurances of pain do not change overnight. Patterns ingrained in us since we were born cannot be unlearned in a matter of days, months, or even years. Working on ourselves and the child within us is not easy, but it is easy to find excuses to not start.

Perhaps a better question to ask is "Will we continue to pass these abusive behaviors on to our children?"

Let's not admit defeat before we even begin. Better said, let's not admit defeat before we reach the end. Progress may be slow and chances may be slim, but there will be no progress and no chance at all if we do not let ourselves try. Maybe the mission we can achieve matters more than the struggles we may endure along the way.

After twenty-one years, I am still unlearning abuse and untangling the knots I made in other relationships. There are times when I reflect on my interactions with others (and myself) and feel an overwhelming wave of anger at how clear it is that I am still affected by my childhood trauma. I cannot run from the fact that I am more of a product of my past than I would like to be. However, I can learn how to give myself the comfort and validation that I am doing my best to break intergenerational chains my previous generations tightened around my family's necks.

JULY 8

11:01 p.m. Today you and I discussed the psychoanalysis of how I receive love based on my upbringing. Accepting and coming to terms with how my past has shaped the way that I am now was hard.

"A person with this [fearful-avoidant] attachment style is confused. They essentially have both the dismissive and the anxious

styles combined—both wanting emotional closeness and also pushing it away. They're fearful of fully trusting others, yet they need approval or validation. They often deny their feelings or are reluctant to express them."

It's hard to accept how true this is. I wish I could say it wasn't, but I guess it is.

JULY 11

10:36 p.m.

My friend mentioned how they seemed to realize a trend in people with my thinking style. I didn't even need to wait for them to finish. I already knew what they would say.

Once again, I believe I am in a gray area because I am someone who is so painfully aware of my depression and self-deprecation that I can identify, observe, and comment on myself like a third party. I know I am someone who—in efforts to push myself away from undesirable characteristics like selfishness, egotism, self-centeredness, greed, and neediness—overcorrects before anything has even happened. This kind of thinking is definitely what I live with when I am depressed. I am so scared of coming off as any of these things that I take steps in advance to prevent it from happening. And it's not even how others perceive me. The harder, more painful part to grasp is that I am trying to prevent myself from seeing me like this. **Of course, because I am hard on myself, I know I will always go further to protect myself from me.** I know this is one of the key problems I have. I know about this, but I struggle to change it.

This all comes down to the core problem that I am so self-deprecating and internalize all fault/responsibility that I am quite hard on myself, believing I can always, always, always be doing better than I am. It's hard. I know this is true, and I've been painfully aware of it for so many years now. Unfortunately, part of depression is that I've completely accepted it as part of me. Is this accepting defeat?

I don't think so. I think it's just accepting me. You can argue that I am completely disillusioned and missing what everyone else is seeing. But I can also argue that I know myself best and only I can make such judgments about myself. You get it. It's an endless cycle. That's why it's so hard to break.

JULY 12
DEPENDENCE
11:18 a.m. We talked about how, growing up, I felt distrust toward my friends. Sure, the sexual assault was a contribution. But the larger reason was that because I was compared so frequently to their successes and put down so often when I was not the same as all of them, I started to feel anger and envy when they did well. I recognized these emotions and it disgusted me that I could feel this way toward my friends, even close ones. I distanced myself from them both in horror of my feelings toward them and in protection of myself from the reasons I had these feelings. He explained to me something I should've seen early on. Because I was cut off from my friends and other people in the world, I became subconsciously dependent on my parents and their words. That's why what they said to me holds such weight. And that's likely why, when I was able to find people outside of them to talk to and share life with, I became very dependent on them. I'm sorry to all of you who have been a product of the displaced trust I've been unable to control.

COINCIDENCE
He told me it's not a coincidence how I react to the world now as a product of my experiences. It's an alignment of factors that makes me who I am. It's not a mere coincidence.

YOU DO NOT NEED
TO HAVE IT ALL
FIGURED OUT
RIGHT NOW

ACCOUNTABILITY

#153: You do not need to have it all figured out right now. Go to sleep, and you can figure it out tomorrow.

I like to think I am responsible for myself. I like to know I am in control of my life, and I am the result of decisions I make for myself. At least, I like to think that.

I spent the last few years researching behavioral economics. This field is the intersection of human psychology and decision-making with economic policy, and it has been endlessly fascinating for me to dive headfirst into its theories and teachings. Regardless of all the niche theories and intricate experiments I learned, one tenet is the single source of truth holding up this whole field: humans are not rational creatures.

While we like to believe we are completely rational, logical, and thoughtful, the truth is we are not always this ideal. We may not always think of our long-term goals and may instead be distracted by short-term desires. You may experience looking back on a past decision and then slapping yourself on the forehead, asking why you made this choice and not another. Of course, everything is crystal clear in hindsight. Unfortunately, as humans, we do not live with the logic and the iron-cold hearts of robots. Instead, we have both our brains and hearts guiding our choices. Therefore, it is not new for me to say we are often incapable of making the purely rational or logical choice.

Our hearts and emotions have a strong foot in the door of decision-making and can interfere. We know that what is good for us may not always be the easiest choice to make. As an example, say it's Sunday night and you have an important deadline at work tomorrow morning. Your boss left on Friday with a firm squeeze on your shoulder, reminding you that he is looking forward to your results on Monday. However, you find yourself in a dilemma on Sunday evening: after a hearty dinner with friends, everyone wants to go to the local comedy club to enjoy the rest of the night. Normally you would be more than happy to entertain this idea, but knowing you lost sleep the past week, it would be incredibly risky to follow your friends for a late night—especially with your 8:00 a.m. call time. You tell yourself you can just set five alarms and you will wake up in time, no problem. You follow your friends. You wake up the next morning at 11:07 a.m. to twelve missed calls from your boss and coworkers. You slap your forehead and ask yourself why you did not make the rational choice last night.

We need to understand that on Sunday evening the rational choice seemed like following your friends. After all, you were happy to be with them and your emotional satisfaction on the weekends is very important. You did not think you would risk oversleeping with five alarms in place and six hours of sleep. It seemed like it would be okay to join the fun. Why didn't things turn out as planned?

As humans, we suffer from the phenomenon of overestimating ourselves. We give ourselves too much credit or believe in ourselves more than we should. Any other person observing such a situation would conclude you should go home early to wake up on time, but you falsely believed you would be capable of waking up despite the past week of sleep deprivation. This phenomenon of overconfidence in our future selves and idealized scenarios causes much regret, and we beat ourselves up after the wrong choices culminate into the wrong outcomes.

How do we, as irrational creatures, make sure we are able to make choices that are as rational as possible? We need to be held accountable.

This accountability comes more naturally to some individuals than others. For those lucky few, all it takes is a few sticky notes posted on their desk. They may not need others to monitor them or to regularly check up on them. Others need a whole squadron of loved ones keeping them accountable to their goals and actions. Regardless, accountability comes when we are prompted by outside cues to keep us on track.

If you tracked your sleep from the previous week and noticed a trend leading to sleep deprivation, you would likely choose to stay at home instead of following your friends. If you kept notes in your phone about why making your deadline matters more than another night in the city, then you would likely choose not to go. If your spouse texted you when it was getting late, then you would likely turn around and wake up refreshed. All these scenarios include an accountability tool.

As irrational creatures, we need support to keep us on track. We need the perspectives of others who are able to see our paths from a different angle so we can make as informed decisions as possible. This means setting reminders for yourself, asking friends for support, or simply practicing daily habits until they become your new normal. We need some way to be held accountable for our actions to see change.

I did not realize how supportive my accountability team would be when I first began creating it. I did not set out to source a handful of my friends to be my accountability team. Instead, it happened in a series of small events. Every time I needed to wake up early for a college final, I texted a friend to call me and make sure I was awake. When I was recovering from anorexia, I asked many of my friends to regularly ask me if I had eaten. I had a rule for myself that I was not allowed to refuse when someone asked me to eat with them. As I reached graduation, I told my partner about the many goals and aspirations I had for myself so we could work on them together. By vocalizing and letting others know about your future and plans, you are held accountable to fulfill them. The more people who know, the better.

Enforcing rules for yourself is also a way to keep yourself accountable through your own means. While it is completely possible for you to be flexible in following your own laws, remind yourself why you set those guidelines in the first place. For example, I know I will not wake up once I drift off into a nap. Therefore, I set a rule: I am not allowed to nap during the daytime so I can have fulfilling rest at the end of the day. While I keep this rule myself, I made sure to write it down so I will regularly see it and also told a few of my friends so they could encourage me to stay away from tempting nap times. By setting guidelines for ourselves, we set up the architecture of staying on our projected pathways.

Right before I began my recovery from anorexia, I told as many people as I could about it. I told my close friends, my international friends, and even friends I had just met. I told my parents, despite it being a very hard conversation. This was my rationale: "Dang it, now everyone knows I struggle with an eating disorder. I need to start working on it once and for all. How can I disappoint all these people who know?" These individuals regularly checked in on me, asked how I was doing, or invited me out to eat with them. What worked for me was that I love these people and I could not disappoint them by not working on my eating disorder. Telling them was the act keeping me accountable. Anything else they did for me was simply their way of showing they were happy to support me.

Without the means to be kept accountable, we often place too much trust in our own inabilities. Our perceptions of the future and reality become biased toward what we want to see, clouding our ability to make rational judgments. We need to practice our own forms of accountability. The following list could help you begin, but like most solutions toward healing, nothing is ever a one-size-fits-all solution. Finding your own accountability tools will be most powerful for continuing your growth.

- Place sticky note reminders around your workspace, bed, and other areas you frequent.
- Let your friends know about your goals and dreams.
- Take notes when you notice yourself slow down so you can identify moments when accountability tools are helpful.
- Ask your family for reminders of things you know you will forget.
- Set alarms throughout the day to get certain things done.

Do not hold yourself back! Keep yourself accountable to keep moving forward in your healing.

ALL WE CAN CONTROL IN OUR LIVES IS OUR MINDSET GOING INTO ANYTHING

CONTROL

#28: All we can control in our lives is our mindset going into anything. Don't try to control what you cannot reach.

"Do you think you have an obsession with control?"

The first time my therapist proposed this thought to me, I instinctively reeled back in horror. I characterize myself as someone with a few screws loose who is playful, silly, and always up for a spontaneous adventure. I welcome the unexpected with open arms and pride myself on not panicking when unknown situations arise.

"Of course not."

I stopped seeing that therapist a few weeks later (for other reasons; I was not *that* disgusted by her proposal of control). A few months later, as I was getting familiar with a new therapist, I was presented with the same question again.

If two different therapists ask you the same question, it's probably worth a second thought.

When I thought of control, I thought of unhealthy scenarios like a possessive lover, a dominating parent, or a power dynamic with a clear inferior party in submission to a superior party. None of these were characteristics I wanted to embody, so control was a word I steered clear of.

Again, I reeled back in horror at the thought of control being a part of who I am. Growing up, control was all I knew. I was raised in environments where control was not mine. The possessive lover, dominating parent, and superior-inferior power dynamic were all present at points in my life, resulting in destructive behaviors. With scars left from each of these during my upbringing, I vowed to never be in controlling relationships again, whether as the controlled or the controller.

A relationship I had not considered, however, was when the two roles exist in the same person as an individual relationship. Maybe it was a good thing my new therapist brought this up with me again.

I often say that when we are pushed forcefully into a corner we bounce back at maximum velocity in the opposite direction. My need for control was that opposite direction I shot toward at maximum velocity. I grew up in uncomfortable situations forcing me to be the controlled party: I was the crying child always afraid of her of parents; I was the lover who was always worried what her partner thought; and I was the product of a society who was never good enough. In these environments, I lacked the liberty to think for myself, much less act for myself. Survival meant pleasing the controller. The situation was unfortunate, but there was no way out. I learned to play the part well—some might say a bit too well.

When I left for college, I was blissfully oblivious to how poorly equipped I was to make my own choices. Feeling like I was able to start a new life for myself half a country away from where I was for the last eighteen years was liberating. I remember journaling and saying this was finally the start to a new life I wanted.

A healthy childhood is on neither end of the control spectrum. Parents should neither fully control a child's life nor give them absolute freedom. Parenting is a fine balance that adjusts over time. When a baby is a newborn, it makes sense for the parents to have more control. After all, the baby cannot yet survive on their own. However, as the baby grows into a child and the child into a teenager, parents start to loosen control in small places here and there so their child learns how to exercise their own control and navigate the consequences that come from their choices. As my therapist discussed with me, a dominating parent who disguises an inability to let go of control as protection for their child will stunt the child's growth. The child does not learn how to control themselves when it has been done for them their whole life.

Control is more than power over another individual. It can be split into control from others and control from self. Someone is the controller and someone is the controlled. Furthermore, there is an additional degree of how much control is exercised. We are used to contexts where control means Person A controls Person B, but less used to Person A controlling Person A. The average healthy individual does not even need to think about the latter situation. If you had an average childhood, your parents slowly released their reigns of control so you could learn to control yourself to the extent that, as an adult, learning control is not something you need to think about. You know when to wake up, how much to eat, when it is appropriate to laugh, and so on. You learned to control yourself well and adapted to your environment as you grew up.

The repercussions of a controlled childhood came out loud and clear in my first year of college. When the floodgates opened and the leashes were released (at least, most of them), I felt free to do what I wanted without the constant watchfulness of the parents and society I left behind.

I controlled my life, and now I was not going to let anyone else control me again.

It makes sense that an individual who was starved for their whole life would immediately leap at an all-you-can-eat buffet with no restriction. Observers would not call this individual a glutton or villainize them. Understandably, this individual is finally receiving a basic human need and is taking in as much as they can to compensate for past deprivation. If we replace "food" with "control" in the same situation, the same logic applies and makes sense.

My buffet was a feast of self-control.

When I was eighteen, in my first year of college, I did not know how to control myself. I did not realize my depravity of self-control would create years of unhealthy habits and anxiety around self-regulation. My desperate grasps for self-control began to bleed out in high school. Sneaking out late at night when my parents were asleep made me feel free, and deliberately choosing what to tell them about my grades and school days were other ways I stole back some control. In college, when my parents were no longer living under the same roof as me, I did not recognize I was standing in front of a buffet of self-control until I had already filled my plate past its capacity.

In my first year of college, I fell into severe anorexia. In high school, my bulimic tendencies were just one of many habits I hid from my parents. When I was no longer in fear of their constant observation, my eating disorder ran free.

The escalation of my eating disorder can be accredited to the buffet of self-control. With a history of sexual assault and rape, I grew up loathing my body and regularly wished it gone. Throwing up my meals was an act of self-control I neither recognized nor knew how to control. The moments I spent hunched over a toilet with sharp stomach pains and a burning throat were acts of defiance against the control I grew up with. This was a part of me my parents did not know and therefore could not control. At the same time, wanting to deprive myself was a control over my body that I had not had during previous traumas.

My anorexia took full effect faster than usual, creating serious physical implications for my well-being—yet, I did not stop. In my head, I needed to lose more and more weight, and I needed to take in as little as possible. This was how I could finally like my body. I ironically set the curve in my freshman biology course about human nutrition and metabolism. I was more than equipped with knowledge about how to care for my body, but none of it was as important to me as controlling my body. That's what made the difference: I confused my control for care.

I find it no surprise that children with parents who are heavy alcoholics are more prone to alcoholism. Putting these children in an environment with free-for-all alcohol would likely be a recipe for disaster. Sometimes explaining my need for self-control as an addiction, like alcoholism, is easier for me. Raised in an environment with parents and a society that exercised full control, it makes sense that I am more prone to having controlling characteristics. Put me in front of a self-control buffet and you won't be able to tell me that you don't expect the same recipe for disaster.

Like most addictions, however, the harmful behavior begins when too much of a good thing becomes a bad thing. Healthy childhoods result in a healthy level of self-control that helps the child navigate their life, but when one is addicted to self-control and cannot loosen their own grip on themselves, then we witness impossibly high expectations, self-punishment, and extremely low self-esteem.

I can't always recognize when my self-control obsession is the underlying cause for my behaviors, but it comes out in little ways. Paired with borderline personality disorder (BPD), my absolute dislike for unknowns is a prime example. A common BPD symptom I carry is seeing the world in black-and-white terms; everything either is or is not. Gray space has no room, and neither do the unknowns in between. After some discussion with my therapist, I was able to see how my black-and-white worldview comes from wanting to gather as much information as I possibly can about any situation so I can feel in control of my responding actions. Lacking certainty of information leads to faulty reactions and less control. Another example is my deliberate choosing of words when I speak. I am careful about each and every word I use since I want to ensure my messages are not lost in translation, controlling the communication as much as possible. Similarly, I see myself and many others carry another unhealthy self-control symptom: giving ourselves impossible expectations and then punishing ourselves when we are unable to reach them, therefore controlling the consequences of our actions or inaction. The list goes on and on until I am unable to control my self-control.

And friends, that is exactly what the answer always is: the control of self-control.

YOU ARE YOUR
PERMANENT HOME

HOME

#110: You are your permanent home. Start taking care of your home.

Little is more comforting than coming home after a long day of work, running errands, and being out and about. If you are as introverted as I am, this is truly what you look forward to—being able to curl up in a space you define as home.

What is a home? You can respond with a lazy Google search and say a home is "the place where one lives permanently, especially as a member of a family or household." Not wrong, but not completely correct by my book either.

I dislike answers that boil down to a trivial, "Well, I guess it depends." I rarely find opportunities when this is both the most appropriate and true answer, but I will give in this one time.

What is a home? Well, I guess it depends.

I would argue that home is more of a feeling than a definition. Perhaps walking into the environment you were raised in feels just like that. Perhaps walking into a space you only became part of in recent months feels more like home. Trying to develop a definition of how a place feels like home, apply it to all future environments, and run the risk of falsely critiquing places with the observation, "This should be my home according to my definition, so why isn't it?" is hardly fruitful.

Luckily, most of us are not so obsessed with defining feelings like this. Most of us.

A house is not always a home, and a home is not always a house. Unlike a home, the definition of a house—a grounded place with four walls and a roof—can be universally defined and agreed upon. The common term for individuals without permanent shelters who survive on the streets is "homeless." While I am not a very political person and will not get into the details, I hesitate when I hear such terms. They may be "homeless," but an observant onlooker may never know. Instead, these individuals are "houseless."

About two years ago, I found myself sitting and contemplating such thoughts. I did not feel at home in the California house in which I spent the first eighteen years of my life, and Chicago was not growing on me either. Aside from questions probing why I did not feel at home in the former despite the unrivaled familiarity I had with the space, I was hit with a revelation I did not welcome: I was homeless.

It never feels good to say we do not feel at home anywhere in the world, but it is another problem if we are not okay with that fact. I could barely sleep when I first came to the realization as I stared at my empty ceiling in the bed I had always known: Was I okay being homeless? Did I want that to change?

While I did not find the answers that night, within a few months the answers came to me. I was okay being homeless. Nevertheless, I wanted it to change.

Remember, most of us are not so obsessed with defining feelings like that. Most of us.

A home is defined differently for each person. After spending too much time thinking about this, I derived five main principles outlining what a home is to me. I do not think I am taking too many liberties in saying these can apply to the rest of the human population as well. With the help of these five principles, I was able to see both how homeless I once was and how all right it was for me to be okay with that now.

1. **Home is where we feel safest.** What causes a permanent house to no longer be a home? I may know every single nook and cranny of the California house I spent my childhood in, but why was this not a home? The simplest answer is that I did not feel safe. Obviously, "safe" is a subjective word each individual could (and should) define on their own. I felt safe because I knew the elements outside would not reach me, the scary dog three houses down would not get to me, and there would always be a bed for me to sleep in. However, those were simply physical definitions of safety.

Safety can be categorized into physical and mental states, and the latter form of safety was greatly lacking for me. I felt like I was always walking through a minefield when I was in the house, my senses on hyperalert for whenever the next explosive fit of anger would shatter the fragile peace. I often felt scared as a middle schooler, dreading the seven-minute walk it took to reach my front door. I did not feel free to be myself, express emotions, and know my true, unapologetic self was welcomed. Without a choice, the house was where I needed to return every night to survive. It was not home. Home is where we can not only safely be ourselves in our purest form but also feel safely accepted as such.

2. **Home is not universal.** The idea of what home is will look largely different from one person to the next, and multiple individuals could live in the same space but not all feel at home. Multiple individuals feeling at home in the same space is a beautiful and wonderful thing, and it's worth noting that everyone occupying the space is part of what makes it home for the others. However, this is something individuals opt into, as opposed to being *assigned* into it. Parents often want their children to feel at home in the space they all share, but the forceful assignment of this desire actually causes the opposite sentiments to develop. Similarly, your home may not feel to your partner how it feels to you, and you have to decide whether you are both okay with that or whether you would like to change it. If we do not feel safe in a place others feel safe in, denying it in order to share a "home" is pointless. It will not be worth it. No one should feel they were assigned their home.

3. **Home does not need to be a place.** Where we feel safest is not always a where, but may be a who, when, or what. A home can be someone with whom you feel most yourself, a time spent on an activity you enjoy most, or an object providing you relief. Home could be a where in which all of these are brought to the same space. Wouldn't that be nice?

4. **You can have multiple homes.** I can only hope we feel safe in more than one instance of our lives.

5. **Your first home should be yourself.** Why am I so obsessed with defining home? My lack of a home was the answer, but an alternative could be that my lack of

security with myself was the answer. A person can't feel at home anywhere else if they are not at home with themselves first. After all, they are the only constant factor in the environments they call home. A home cannot exist if the very being occupying it does not feel safe with themselves. No matter where the individual goes, they will not feel safe.

I purposely avoided parts of myself which I wanted to hide and turned a blind eye to ugly traumas. Instead of accepting these as parts of me which I was still working on, I chose not to know who I was and, in turn, not feel safe with myself. I was homeless. When I began to finally find home in myself, I was okay with not having a home anywhere else; I already had one and that was more than I thought I would ever have. It took longer than I would like to build a home within myself, but I have yet to find a place, a person, an action, an item, or anything else accepting me for my purest self as I do. I'm okay with that. Now I have myself.

A home is not a place we can control. Maybe Google was right about one thing: homes are meant to be permanent. They are meant to be permanent, not in the sense of withstanding the trials of time but in the sense that we do not believe homes will leave us anytime soon. We move houses and locations to keep up with the hustle and bustle of life, and we leave behind places once called home. Coming back to them later, these places may or may not be home to us anymore. However, in the moments when they were home, we did not think about when that would no longer be the case. Home was permanent because it was home for as long as we were there.

It makes sense to make our first home ourselves. We must be our permanent safe place.

YOU DO NOT HAVE
ENOUGH TIME IN
THIS WORLD TO
BE DROPPING
HINTS ABOUT
WHAT YOU NEED

BOUNDARIES

#57: You do not have enough time in this world to be dropping hints about what you need. Speak your boundaries.

Humans are some of the most fragile animals on this planet. It would be nice if we had a scaly exoskeleton or poison to keep predators away, but instead, we got stuck with squishy skin and subpar speed. We have boundaries for practically everything—on the highways, in the skating rink, at the Grand Canyon, and on escalators. These boundaries save more than a handful of lives every year.

I thought we would be better at setting boundaries around our hearts by this point. Our ribs can only do so much.

I sent the text and slumped against the window. My eyes glazed over, not focusing on anything but still more alert than I would have liked.

I fall on the "more fragile" than the "less fragile" side of our species. If you are anything like me, you tend to learn your lessons only after you are burned. I did not start wearing my helmet until an ugly bike tumble down the street, and I did not understand how much anorexia ate at my body until I landed in a hospital with a malfunctioning heart.

Unfortunately, most of the human population falls into this "more fragile" group when it comes to setting boundaries.

Personal boundaries are the limits we set for ourselves in our relationships, including how we interact with both others and ourselves. They are how we protect our hearts when our ribs can only do so much. A person with healthy boundaries can say "no" when they want to, and another person with healthy boundaries can say "yes" to the same. Like how each of us have different spice tolerances, each of us also have different boundaries. Wherever we set our boundaries is completely up to us and what our thresholds are. Having stricter or looser boundaries is not for anyone but us to comment on. We are not born with control over how many spicy peppers we can down in one sitting, yet our spice tolerance can be adjusted if we train ourselves. Boundaries are no different.

And, for most of us, we set our boundaries too loosely—until we get hurt.

I heard the buzzing of my phone against my pocket and saw a notification that my friend responded to my message. It was nearly 2:00 a.m. and I was in a taxi headed toward my apartment. My hands shook. I looked out the window at the lights of a familiar road speeding by. One last second, and I'll open the message. At least, that's what I told myself. Seconds became minutes, and we rounded the corner before reaching my building. I climbed out, holding back tears but managing to muster a "thank you" to the polite driver.

Unlike physical pain, we do not always recognize emotional pain. Sometimes we realize our hurt after the fact and sometimes we do not ever realize it. While ignorance is bliss, a breach of our boundaries affects more than what we are conscious of. Like an infectious disease inside our bodies, noticing the symptoms may be too late when the disease has already taken hold of our vital organs.

Were the stairs up always this long? Were my shoes always this heavy? Before I was aware of it, I took off my shoes, locked the door behind me, and crawled into bed. Never mind that I had not changed or showered. I thought I wanted nothing more than to shower away this feeling, but I guess I was wrong. I wanted nothing more than to curl up and cry. I did not know how to feel. I did not know what I was feeling. Maybe that was for the better in this moment.

Setting boundaries for ourselves means we are able to shake our heads and turn down what we do not want, yet also means being comfortable with opening ourselves up a bit more for our closer relationships. It might be difficult for us to always recognize when it is time to put a boundary between ourselves and others. We might be scared that turning down a dinner invitation for much-needed alone time will be seen as inconsiderate and selfish, so we accept, show up, and go home at the end of the night feeling burned out. We confuse where boundaries should be by negotiating ours for the consideration of others. More often than not, the impact of these sacrifices is not realized until you are already burned out at home, full from dinner yet drained inside. Setting up boundaries for ourselves is not selfish at all. No one can fault you for wanting to care for yourself first before others.

When you set boundaries, do not risk yourself by setting up looser boundaries than you can tolerate. Do not believe it is worth being burned before learning where your boundaries are.

It was my fault I felt like this, though. I should not have been so naive. I should not have been alone with him. I should not have thought he was going to be as friendly to me as he had been these last few months. Who was I kidding? How would I have known?

Like anything else in this world, boundaries must have balance. If we keep boundaries too tight around our hearts, we miss out on opportunities to develop close relationships. If we keep them too loose, we make ourselves prone to having them bent by those who do not have our best intentions in mind. Furthermore, we have different boundaries set for different parts of our lives. The way we interact with our partner is different from how we interact with coworkers, which is then different from how we interact with family.

Defined boundaries are what keep your relationships in your life.

I mean, I did what I could, right? I told him no. But maybe it was my fault I did not say no one more time. Or a few more times. Or enough times until he stopped.

When we set boundaries too tightly, we avoid opportunities to develop close relationships and intimacies. Everything is kept within us, and we do not share our joys or difficulties with the world. We are unable to ask for help and struggle to do everything ourselves when we are unable to show others our struggles. Those around us are kept at a distance to minimize the possibility of rejection. We keep ourselves thorny so no one can reach in and touch us.

On the other side, when our boundaries are too loose, we give too much to others and keep less for ourselves. We might overshare personal information or find it difficult to say "no" to requests, causing us to support others more than we do ourselves. We become dependent on others' opinions and fear their rejection because our days are defined by everyone else. Our hearts are left in the open, letting abuse and disrespect in more easily when the doors are not locked.

It was my fault. I should have screamed. I should have been louder. I should have . . . I should have done so much more. I should have said no again. But why did the first one not matter? Never mind. It was my fault I didn't say it louder, didn't say it more firmly, didn't say it again . . . it was my fault. I should have said something, anything. But I didn't. Couldn't? Wouldn't. My desire to not cause a scene with my friend was stronger, I guess. Would anyone have even heard me? Would it have done anything? Would anyone have been able to interfere? I should have interfered. I should have stopped it. I didn't. And that's on me.

Do not wait to set your boundaries until after you are hurt. Be proactive and not reactive in the protection of your heart. That said, setting your boundaries late is still better than never. But where do we start?

Boundaries, unlike guardrails we see on the highways, in the skating rink, at the Grand Canyon, or on escalators, are meant to be flexible. They are meant to change as we grow and gather experiences guiding our tolerance levels.

Start by knowing what healthy boundaries look like. Healthy boundaries allow us to value our own opinions while knowing how to engage in conversations with those who hold different opinions. We do not compromise our values for others, and we also know how much to share of ourselves when appropriate. With healthy boundaries, we know what we need and can communicate our needs because we feel respected and can have a discussion if someone speaks up and disagrees with us.

Oftentimes, we do not recognize boundaries in our lives since we do not even think about them. If the boundaries are doing their job and keeping us protected, then it makes sense to keep them where they are. Healthy boundaries lead to healthy relationships, so imagine those you have healthy relationships with. What kinds of practices make them healthy? Why do you feel safe in those relationships? What do you do, and what do they do, to support the relationship together?

And I hated that. But it's my fault, anyway. I let myself be in that situation. I let myself not say no.

While boundaries exist in every relationship we have, they come in multiple forms depending on the nature of the relationship. We have multiple boundaries in each relationship and each boundary is as important as the last. When evaluating the relationships we have, realize that our boundaries can change from person to person. They come in many shapes and forms—intellectual, emotional, physical, and more—but it is completely up to us which ones we keep with whom.

If you feel like you need to sit down with someone and have a discussion about your boundaries, make it happen earlier rather than later. A conversation about boundaries is not pushing others away by setting barriers around yourself. Instead, it encourages others and shows that you would like to develop a healthy relationship. Keep the people in your life who can understand this and be enthusiastic about discussing your boundaries.

I looked at my phone. I looked at the notification for a few long seconds before opening the message.

The right people in our lives will never ask about our boundaries or why they are there. They will not question whether our boundaries are too rigid; they will respect that there is a reason for where our boundaries are set. We do not owe them an explanation. They will never make us feel bad or selfish for choosing to keep our boundaries where we feel safe, so we should not make ourselves feel bad or selfish either. The right people in our lives will make us want to loosen our boundaries with them at the same pace they do. No boundaries were ever taken down without being established first.

Set your boundaries closer to your heart than further, but allow them to be flexible for when it feels safe. There is no blame when you take care of you.

"*Emily, that's not your fault. That's called rape.*"

JULY 11
ASSAULT

1:57 p.m. I was talking to you about my previous experiences regarding sexual assault and other forms of contact that made me averse to physical contact for a long period of my life. You were telling me, like everyone else does, that I seem to be really strong. **I shrug it off all the time because, really, it feels like it doesn't matter much to me.** However, I had to think again.

Am I able to shrug it off because I was able to get over that bump in my life? Because I was able to recover? Aside from one instance in particular, I feel like all the previous experiences I have with assault would traumatize most females, but they were genuinely experiences that bothered me for a day or two. Then, I just moved on. So I don't think this is it.

Was I able to shrug it off because I'm so incredibly desensitized to such experiences? If so, what does that say about my coping mechanisms? Have I always been someone who feels like I just shut down and move all the negative emotions from my head? Is that really a way I should be coping?

Or is it simply that I am someone who does not react to external effects? I know I am someone who reacts more when I know something was caused by me or was my fault. When I feel like these "bad events" happen to me outside of my control, I just don't react as much. What does this say about me and how much of an imbalance this implies? If any of my friends were to have the same experiences as I did, I would instantly jump in to help them. But when it comes to me . . . I just shrug them off. I think I really am someone who puts a lot on myself. The events in my life that have affected me in the past are events I feel I was responsible for, or which I had some degree of control in.

I'm sure this is something I need to work on.

BOUNDARIES

2:37 a.m. Thank you for being someone whom I have always been able to talk about anything and everything with. You were the first person I was able to talk to about many of my issues around anorexia and the first person with whom I was able to openly discuss the thought processes I felt the rest of the world would judge. You're so strong. **You say you admire me, but I admire you. Isn't that beautiful?**

Thank you for telling me tonight that you were not comfortable talking about this topic with me when I was emotional. It takes a lot to be able to tell someone when you are unable to help them. I find that to be such beautiful strength. Thank you for putting yourself first. Thank you for recognizing you are not in a place where you can help me. Thank you for letting me know and not straining yourself. I am so grateful you let me know. I admire that so much in you: you know your boundaries and can let me know. Please don't say sorry. Please take care of yourself, and thank you for turning me away but trusting I will be able to help myself without you.

DO NOT EVER
FEEL BAD FOR
DOING WHAT IS
BEST FOR YOU

COPING MECHANISMS

#152: Do not ever feel bad for doing what is best for you.

You didn't need to take candy from me as a small child to make me cry; I would cry over just about anything. Even now, I have a hard time controlling those emotions, but you won't see me throwing tantrums anymore (if you take candy from me, that might be a different story).

Small children throw temper tantrums when, deep inside, they feel so much frustration, anger, or sadness that the only way they know to express themselves is through an outburst of emotion. We don't see adults throw temper tantrums (at least, not as often as we see small children do). This is not to say adults no longer feel the same kinds of frustration, anger, or sadness anymore. Rather, we have been taught to develop and have adapted to a greater capacity to withstand the effects of these emotions on ourselves. We are able to better control ourselves and cope when negative emotions overwhelm us.

What has not changed since we were small children is that we still have limits. Thresholds within us can, when trespassed, evoke reactions or outbursts atypical for us. Common examples you have likely witnessed include:

- Road rage after a stressful day of work
- Dropping everything to get a midnight burger after nonstop studying for twelve hours the night before your final exam
- Spending your entire month's savings online shopping after a particularly bad argument with a significant other

All of these examples occur after a buildup of detrimental emotion which finally reaches a tipping point. Those of us who find ourselves trapped in our own minds feel like we are boiling over inside, like we don't know when we will blow the fuse that keeps everything together. It feels like we're hanging by a thread before snapping and acting irrationally.

When life is better for us, we may look back at these outbursts and wonder what drove us to such dramatic actions. We shake our heads at our past selves, shaming ourselves or feeling embarrassed for how we dealt with those emotions. The truth is that we each have coping mechanisms we turn to. However, we may not be aware of our own habits and coping mechanisms.

I began my habits of self-harm during my middle school years, around age eleven. I cannot explain how I feel in those moments when I have the controlling urge to relieve myself of the chaos inside my head. Sometimes it feels like I am in absolute paralysis until I just get rid of everything inside me. So many voices from myself overwhelm me. In those moments, I want nothing more than to get it all out. I found the fastest means for me to snap out of those moments was self-harm, from stabbing myself to binge eating. None of these habits were good for me, and I knew it. I continued them because they were the only way I knew to cope. My emotions overwhelmed me so much that I would rather hurt myself in the moment to break away from my own thoughts than work on long-term solutions. I continued these habits for over eight years.

It may be difficult for some of us to notice which of our habits can be categorized as coping mechanisms. Stripped down, coping mechanisms are actions we turn to as our own way of temporarily escaping from overwhelming emotions. Often, this is all they offer—a temporary escape. Ideally, we would be able to face whatever is causing us the tension or anxiety in our lives and address it. However, this ideal does not always exist when we want it to.

In order to work on your coping mechanisms, you need to be in a headspace of not currently relying on coping mechanisms. As you work through the following exercises, you should be calm enough to be truthful about your habits and experiences.

Deep down, you'll know if you're ready.

The first step is identifying the coping mechanisms you already turn to. I generally recommend journaling or writing during these moments so you can later revisit the thoughts overwhelming you as well as the urges you had. Journaling slows down the onset of negative emotions' reliance on coping mechanisms. By writing, you force yourself to put your thoughts into language and words on paper. The longer thoughts are kept in the nebulous depths of your head, the easier it is for them to grow too intense for you to deal with. Journaling and putting them into words pins them down. Try it next time.

After you detect a coping mechanism, you need to categorize whether it is worth keeping. Once again, coping mechanisms should not be permanent solutions to your problems. They are temporary escapes from reality. Until you are able to find lifelong solutions to your stressors, healthy coping mechanisms can support you. It may be hard to understand whether or not they are healthy. Sometimes, what feels good is not what is best. This is why these exercises need to be done when you are in a calm headspace and can be honest with yourself about whether you feel good about your coping mechanisms. If you find this difficult, reach out to a friend or a trusted individual whose judgment you trust.

Unhealthy coping mechanisms include:

- Marinating in your thoughts
- Hurting yourself
- Throwing things, even pillows, against walls
- Screaming out the window
- Binge eating until you feel like bursting
- Driving fast without care
- Drinking alcohol
- Taking out your emotions on the people around you
- Healthy coping mechanisms include:
- Doing yoga to calming music
- Journaling happy memories from the day
- Creating a to-do list for a day you're looking forward to
- Planning your next outing with friends
- Taking a warm shower or bath
- Changing your outfit to look good
- Cooking a new recipe you've been dying to try
- Going on a light jog to take in your surroundings
- Anything else in your life that does not distract you from the problem but helps you handle your reaction to it

If you find your coping mechanisms are not healthy for you, then it is time to start working on them. Identify other activities in your life that are able to completely focus your mind. After all, the purpose of coping mechanisms is to distract us from our overwhelmingly negative emotions by turning our attention somewhere else until the storm passes. This could include finishing schoolwork, cleaning your space, going on a walk, watching videos of ASMR baking, baking said ASMR recipe, or calling a friend. These are habits you should be working on shifting toward. Choose a handful to start with.

Habits are not built in a day—especially not in a day when you turn to other habits during overwhelming stress. To truly instill healthy coping mechanisms in your life, you need to replace the unhealthy negative habits with new healthy habits. You need to start incorporating the healthy habits into your daily life even when you don't find yourself in need of them—even when you are doing just fine. When you turn to coping mechanisms, rationally telling yourself to try a new healthy habit for the first time is impossible. Make it easier for yourself to turn to new habits in the future by giving yourself a push earlier on and making healthy habits a regular part of your day now.

At the same time, however, we must all give ourselves courtesy and respect when we turn to less-than-ideal coping mechanisms. In hard moments, my first thoughts are never "How do I healthily help myself in this situation?" but "How do I help myself in this situation?" Sometimes I find myself suddenly faced with an anxiety-inducing situation forcing me to react immediately. If I'm unable to calm myself down with healthy coping mechanisms due to the volatility of the situation, then the best I can do is a less-than-ideal solution. For example, instead of calming my breathing by counting in my head, I might end up walking out of the situation to remove myself, which just puts the problem out of sight. When I am in a better headspace, I'll beat myself up for not controlling myself better. It hurts me to know others experience the same thing.

Temporary Band-Aids, while not the most adhesive, are still Band-Aids offering protection when we are under threat. We do not need to beat ourselves up for reaching out for the protection of Band-Aids when we are unable to protect ourselves. No one will blame another for "not controlling themselves better" when they need a Band-Aid to patch up a bleeding cut before they can have a healing ointment. No one will blame another for protecting themselves. What matters is staying safe in unsafe situations, and Band-Aids do a damn good job of that.

Coping mechanisms, no matter how perfect or healthy they are, have limitations. They may not always be regularly available or accessible based on your environment, or they may not bring you the same type of calm relaxation for every situation (coping mechanisms are not a one-size-fits-all). Sometimes, they can even lead to new kinds of stress. Other times, they lose their magic due to being overused. Therefore, an arsenal of mechanisms you can turn to and cycle through as needed is necessary. Becoming reliant on one mechanism is unhealthy for your future self should it become unavailable. Have safety nets for your safety net.

If you find the healthy coping mechanism you are trying to build into your life is not feasible, then move on to trying the next one. What is most important is that you are continuously identifying unhealthy habits, trying healthy alternatives, and working on replacing unhealthy habits with healthy relief. Go get that healthy coping mechanism.

Changing your unhealthy habits into healthier channels of relief brings you halfway there but is still reliance on coping mechanisms. Working on them means you are able to patch up a leak every time there is a new hole, but you also want to stop the holes from being punched in the first place. Your shiny, new healthy coping mechanisms are temporary support so you can reach long-term healing: to be at a place where anxieties and stressors no longer turn you toward them.

We all feel like small children with explosive temper tantrums at times. Coping mechanisms deserve our time and space to be useful, and we deserve respect throughout the process. Even Band-Aids can stop leaks from growing into floods.

AUGUST 30

1:02 p.m. We're in the midst of moving, so there has been a lot of cleaning out. I found some of my old diet pills. They stopped working on me. I had taken them too often. But I kept them.

I know they're a crutch for me—an easy way out, an easy way for me to hurt myself. I know I need to work on it. I am. I know when I'm in a bad place the easiest way for me to calm down is by hurting myself. I know when I'm not okay I feel like I need to punish or hurt myself to make things more okay. But I also know how much these habits have hurt me, both inside my body and outside, on my skin. And somehow, I found comfort in pills I knew would force my body to deeper points of deprivation and starvation. I shouldn't say "somehow." I know why.

I threw them away today. Are you proud of me? I'm not sure if I'm proud of myself. It felt like I was throwing away something that was familiar, safe, and stable to me. Something I relied on. I'll learn to stand on my own two feet soon, right?

YOU HAVE NOT
YET MET ALL OF
THE PEOPLE WHO
WILL FALL IN
LOVE WITH YOU

LOVELESS

#202: You have not yet met all of the people who will fall in love with you. Why not start with getting to know yourself?

You know how much I dislike those "Live, Laugh, Love" home decorations I see in every suburban mall? Probably more than I really should, but I'm not keeping track.

You know how many failed relationships I've had? Probably more than I really should, but I'm not keeping track.

A therapist I had when I was going through one of my toughest years told me his diagnosis for me was self-love deficiency. I did not fully understand it at the time. Many of my friends already told me I do not love myself enough, but he told me I did not love myself at all.

It did not make sense to me. I do not mean self-love. I mean love.

I often say, "I don't know what I don't know." This is not false, yet it also means I would not know what I did not know even if I came in contact with it. Out of everything I don't know about in this world, love is the one that has confused me the most.

A child's first interaction with love comes from their parents and family. When we are first born, we are blank slates knowing only what we interact with. It makes sense that children learn love through watching their parents interact and how their parents interact with them. Understanding that a child who grows up in a household with fighting parents will struggle with love is not rocket science.

Yet, it was rocket science for me to understand I am that child.

Love is easier to break than to fix. In some of the ugliest fights I had with my parents, they asked why I could only remember the bad, not the good. I didn't want to remember the fights, the screaming, and all the trauma. I know there were good times when we went out for burgers and fries on rare weekend lunches, when I fell asleep on the way home to the sound of pattering rain against the window and the slow humming of the car. I remember bits of joy, like when I was allowed to go up and down aisles of a bookstore as my parents shopped for groceries next door. I walked out more often than not with a new book I was so eager to read. Nonetheless, there were also nights when I went to sleep to the sound of my struggling breaths over a rainstorm outside, or when thrown books slammed against walls as I cowered in the corner of my closet underneath hanging coats. I would not choose to remember these darkened memories if it were up to me. I really wouldn't.

If you ask my friends what kind of person I am, the common answer will be how much of a mother I am to them. I enjoy caring for them, cooking them dinners, or bringing (dragging) them home after parties and tucking them all into bed. Some of my favorite memories are times when it was expressed to me that my concern for everyone's well-being was truly appreciated. I am always more than happy to go out of my way to make someone else smile, whether that be with small gifts that made me think of them, checking in during a bad day, or delivering food for a busy friend. I try my hardest to be a safe space for the people in my life. It's become something I take pride in.

I also still struggle to do it for myself.

I first heard this characterization of me in my high school debate team. I stepped down from my team captain position after junior year but still hung around the officer team since we were all friends. Throughout my senior year, I made an effort to still show up to meetings, coach the underclassmen, bring snacks to tournaments, and boost team morale. During the senior officer banquet nearing graduation, my name was read out loud and a silence took over the room when the advisor asked through the microphone, "Huh, what officer position is Emily?" I felt myself chuckle. I was still associated with the officer team despite stepping down a year ago. From the crowd, one of the underclassmen yelled out, "Team mom!" The advisor laughed, nodded, and proceeded: "Right, team mom. Emily's team mom."

That same underclassman texted me a few years later when I was in college. They took up the role of captain after me and did a much better job than I did.

"You've been such a brave and kind person. It takes a super big heart to be able to take a broken team and to slowly weave it back together again, and to support its members through thick and thin. This year as captain I found myself thinking many times, 'What would Emily do?' and I can't wait to see what you do next year!"

I still read that text on days when I need to show love to myself. If three different therapists and all of your close friends tell you that you suck at loving yourself, maybe there is at least a hint of truth to it.

Love is not unidirectional. It needs to be given and received. Love cannot be received if it has not been given, and love cannot be given if it will not be received. Love exists in relationship, not in isolation.

I always thought I was really good at caring for others. I had no problem pouring my heart out to the people around me. For a period of my life, I felt my happiness came from the happiness of those I care for. But I'm human too.

Love does not make sense to me. It really does not.

I did not grow up feeling love or knowing what love looked like. My memories fail to help me receive love from the people and environment all children ought to receive love from first. After a child has built their foundation of love from their parents and family, they build their ability to love themselves in healthy progression. Next, they are able to love others and share that love in balance between themselves and others.

If we do not even have the first steps, unsurprisingly, the following ones cannot be pursued.

One of my therapists believed that I am still at a five-year-old's level of understanding love. I did not develop the ability to receive love from family, from myself, or from others. He was right: I have difficulty accepting compliments or thinking I deserve care. I cried when a partner's mother once gave me chocolates for my birthday because I did not know how to handle those emotions. Like a wall, I stopped any incoming care from reaching my heart. Letting that wall down was difficult when I was raised and conditioned to keep it up at all times with those I was supposed to receive love from first. I could not understand how to receive the love and care I so readily and happily gave to others.

Although I have difficulty accepting love, I know I give it out more freely than most. Compassion and empathy are character traits close to my heart and my identity, and it fills me with so much joy when I am able to care for others. How and why is this the case?

The answer is deceptively simple. I have an unhealthy relationship with love.

Humans are social animals. Living in isolation from one another is difficult, and the way we are able to coexist stems from invisible contracts between groups of people granting mutual dependency and support. In short, humans are made to care for each other much like other social animals. We are made for care and love to be part of our lives.

Due to my lack of love from others, I filled my need for love by giving it. I kept love present in my life by sending it out to those I care about. This was a blessing in disguise.

Imagine the love in each person's life as a bottle. The bottle needs to be filled up, but how we fill it is up to us. Healthy individuals know for themselves how to balance its ingredients. For some, it might mean filling it up more with love received than love given. Others could have the opposite recipe. What is constant between those with healthy relationships with love is their mix of both receiving and giving love, not just one or the other. My bottle is filled up with love given and no love received.

I thought it was okay as long as my bottle was filled up. I felt like I was happy and I had a very loving lifestyle caring deeply for others. However, my happiness soon became defined by how others felt. Instead of going out of my way to care for them, I was making sacrifices of my own well-being. I started feeling responsible for how those around me felt. When others tried to step in and care for me, I did not know how to accept it and refused it.

While I might still be at a five-year-old's level of understanding love, the rest of my life has not stopped moving forward. I am no longer in the stage where I can develop loving relationships with my parents and family. That chapter is closed, and I am okay walking away from it. My growth was stunted as I moved onto the next chapter (which, according to my therapist, was the twelve-year-old level): learning to love myself.

When we are unable to receive love for ourselves, we lack motivation to give it. This cycle is harmful and feeds itself, and eventually we come to the conclusion that love for oneself is fruitless and should not even be attempted. After all, my bottle was full from loving others, and I was happy there. I was content.

I was content for years, but I was not happy for longer. Deep relationships I developed became unhealthy when I was unable to take care of my well-being in exchange for theirs. I was hurt when partners I loved deeply gave me scars I could not heal because I never learned to treat myself. The self-destructive cycle of my recipe became clearer and clearer, but my addiction to loving others and putting others first prevented me from seeing the reality.

I always loved romance stories. I love watching those silly romance comedy movies we all know could never happen in reality, where the lead characters are swept away on some fantastical, romantic adventure. I gave so much of myself to my partners to watch them be happy. I loved "love."

And that should have been the earliest warning sign of my self-love deficiency.

That was a particularly tough year for me. Amid a suicide attempt, a breakup, and rape, I was still blind to my lack of self-love. Even when my close friends became angry at me for blaming myself for the rape, I was blinded. Even when I told myself to work on my mental health for the sake of keeping my boyfriend, I was blinded. Even when I stood on the edge of a cliff late one night and blamed myself for the destruction of my own life, I was blinded. And even then, it was not enough for me to realize the problem hid in my inability to love myself.

A year later, I was still in similar situations. An unwelcome déjà vu becoming a sort of cycle my friends and therapist witnessed. The unhealthy relationships I landed in time and time again with friends, boyfriends, and family reached a point that was too much for me to bear. Out of sheer desperation for my sanity, I removed myself from everyone in my life.

Finally, I was alone with myself—just me in this great big world.

I did not know what I was doing, and I did not know what the next steps were. All I knew was I could not handle relationships at that point. I could not handle being with others, but the real question was whether I could handle being alone with my own mind.

I did not have a choice. After all, all we have is ourselves. I am glad I did not have a choice.

I was always scared of who I was on the inside, unable to allow myself to be alone for extended periods of time out of fear. I filled my days with time with others. I couldn't tell if I truly enjoyed it or if they were simply distractions and excuses to prevent me from being alone. I was scared, terrified even, of the person I would find if I were alone.

To keep a long story shorter, I began to love myself in isolation.

With a new therapist, I shared this journey and the progress I was making. I told her one session that I was not ready to let others back into my life yet, especially those I cared a lot about. I was scared of returning to what was once familiar to me, pouring all of my love into them instead of myself simply because I care for them so much. I told her that until I was able to give and receive love, I was not going to let others come back into my life.

She laughed. I was startled. Did my master plan not sound healthy? It sure sounded healthy for me. Heck, I was even proud of it. And here she was, laughing!

She reminded me I was losing sight again. Learning to love does not happen in neat, orderly partitions, nor is it as easy as closing a chapter and opening a new one. It did not make sense to suddenly reintroduce people into my life and expect myself to know how to deal with love in relationships all at once. It also did not make sense to keep my walls closed until I was "ready" to be in loving relationships after I had sufficient self-love.

We are only human. We will always be learning how to love ourselves and others. We give some, we lose some, but we win some and we take some. There is no clear step-by-step manual. Instead, we have a general pathway with signposts to guide the journey. As I was learning to love myself, to give and receive love with myself, I needed to slowly reintroduce people into my life to learn how to balance the two ingredients in my bottle. If I suddenly emptied half of a bottle now filled with self-love to fill the rest up with love with others, too much would splash out. A healthy relationship with love means we can grow the size of our bottle through growing our love for ourselves at the same time as growing our love for others, with neither at risk of pushing the other out.

Are we ready to love others? I do not know if there is a point of readiness, and that is why our bottles are simply filled, never capped to change.

JULY 8
11:37 a.m. A quote from a friend made me cry inside:

"But I also think the less you love yourself the lower
your standards are for other people loving you. If you
only love yourself 10 percent and someone comes along
and loves you 10 percent, you'll be shocked."

Their words are so true. It hurt to realize I was blind to it. Yet I still loved and love you when I know I'm not 100 percent.

I always felt like you gave me so much more love than I've felt my whole life. I wonder what my percentage of self-love was and how much that took from me.

"Well if you think about it and you only have
10 percent of your own heart filled up

And he gives you even like 5 percent of his

And you lose 5 percent, you are going to feel like you lost a lot

When in reality it's a tiny amount

If you love yourself 100 percent, no matter how much you lose you will still be satisfied."

GIVE AND TAKE

5:59 p.m. Yesterday you asked me how I could be so nurturing and warm toward my friends when growing up this was exactly what I lacked. I did not know how to answer. It would be logical for someone who grew up with a lack of something to be unable to give it to others, but in my case it seems to have been the opposite. I am able to give so much of something I lack. At the very core of it, all I know is that being nurturing and warm toward people in my life makes me happy. It makes me happy to give this. It makes me happy when I make others happy. And my therapist theorizes this is because I was so devoid of it that subconsciously I never wanted to be devoid of it again. Until I was able to receive this from others, I could make it rich in my life through giving it. I know I have a problem receiving love and affection without discounting its value for myself. I'm working on it. But until then, I may make my life rich and meaningful by giving love to others.

MATTER

2:45 a.m. Thank you for dealing with me today when I asked so many questions. Thank you for responding back when I was invalidating myself. I still find it impossible to completely believe what you said. I cannot bring myself to ask anything from anyone. I don't feel like I deserve to ask anyone to do anything for me, to do anything to make me happy. Who am I to ask from others? I don't mind if I'm not receiving. I've always been a giver. I'm happy giving. I don't feel right asking.

"You're telling yourself you don't deserve these things, but you do. Because you can't be giving more than you're getting. I really need you to know it's okay to expect things from a person. Your needs are the most important here."

"Why is that? I don't feel like these are even needs. These are just useless wants. I'm just honestly more upset at myself for feeling like this."

"Because you matter. You're a giver. You matter to me."

AUGUST 27
9:27 p.m. This made me laugh so much. Love you too.

"You scare me as a human being. I don't know how I feel about your existence."

BIRTHDAY
11:04 p.m. **Today I was reminded there are parts of me I think I know about but truly don't.** I'm still surprised about what I learn about myself.

I've always chosen to not tell people when my birthday is. I don't really celebrate it. I love celebrating my friends' birthdays and always go all-out to shower them in happiness. However, when it comes to myself, I don't want to have anything done on the day. I just want it to pass like another day.

Today I learned why.

I'm still learning how to react to care and love. I don't know what to do when someone shows me care. I don't know how to feel when someone shows me love. I remember this past birthday, when your mom gave me some chocolates for a gift, all I could do was sit and cry with you because I didn't know how to feel. That act alone felt like a lot more love and care than I can remember on this *day every year. I don't know what to do when people around me celebrate for me or show me they care. I don't know how to react. I don't know what to do.*

I didn't grow up in an environment where I was given love and care when I needed it, much less when I needed it most. I grew up devoid and starved. My therapist is still figuring out why I am able to give so much love and care now when I had no access to it as a child. My theory is that I want to have love and care in my life, and because I do not know how to accept it, the way I am able to have it is by giving it to everyone.

The reason I don't like to celebrate my birthday is because I don't know how to feel if people celebrate me. *I only feel overwhelmed by their love and just . . . don't know how to feel. I would just cry.*

LOVE YOURSELF
ENOUGH TO KNOW
WHEN ENOUGH IS
ENOUGH

OPTIMIZATION

#42: Love yourself enough to know when enough is enough.

"You just think you're perfect, don't you?" My therapist really has such a way with words. It catches me off guard. I look at her smile, then back at my feet, then back at her.

"Sorry, I don't think I understand what you're trying to say."

"I'm not trying to say anything. You just think you're perfect, right?" I watched her face. Was there a catch? Her smile didn't change.

Confused as I was, I kept my composure. She couldn't be serious. She had witnessed hours of conversations in which I was unable to build up self-esteem or struggled to figure out why I was worth existing. I wished I thought I was perfect. That would make life much easier.

"You think you're perfect and everything in your life will go exactly how it's playing out in your head. You've given yourself expectations you think you could meet if you approached situations differently. But in reality, we have no way to prove it. And you beat yourself up over hypotheticals."

As much as I thought I could read her, she could read me better.

Truly, we should marvel at the advancements of civilization, which allow us to be where we are today. When survival was no longer our main priority, we were able to explore channels of communication, innovations to build shelters, and strategies to maximize our lifespans. This evolved us to the present, where each of us have opportunities if we just look around us.

And, at the same time, it made humans the most anxious species on Earth.

Anxiety levels reach new peaks each year. Even with our minds no longer stuck in survival, we are not worry-free. Instead, we find new anxieties to worry over. When "nothing is impossible" becomes the mantra of the century, "everything is possible" is its counterpart. This has evolved into "everything should be done." With rising expectations and seemingly no limit to what we can achieve, one can see how anxiety picks away at our brains.

Anxiety blurs lines with regret when we fall victim to our own fantasies. When we look back on something that went wrong in the past, we find holes to poke at and blame ourselves. All of a sudden, everything is within our responsibility and control. "If only I did this differently, then the results would have been more favorable." "Man, I should have chosen the other option instead, that would have saved me more time." "I knew I shouldn't have rushed. I'd have done a better job." The anxieties are ruthless and endless.

I am more than guilty of living in these fantasies. In fact, for most of us with anxiety, it would not be a stretch to say we are fueled by our beliefs and regrets from each instance when we could have done better but did not. It becomes a dangerous trap when we allow ourselves to scrutinize every single choice we made, poking holes not only in places where things could have gone *more* to plan but also poking where things could have gone *better*.

These anxieties are so dangerous because of how easily they can overwhelm us. When every step we take is shrouded in microanalysis, we leave no breathing room for ourselves. We become scared of making decisions in the future due to the possible regrets we know can come later, or we become caught up in rash attempts to understand the results of every possible outcome before we ultimately choose a course of action. Both are forms of paralysis—the inability to make a choice out of fear, and the inability to make a choice out of an insatiable search for more information.

Perhaps this will be the downfall of mankind—our inability to make informed decisions we will not regret.

Such anxieties are fueled by a key flaw in human nature: our overconfidence in limited assumptions.

While this flaw originally helped our species survive, it has not been able to evolve accordingly with the rest of society. Instead, it evolved much too quickly. When we were still hunter-gatherers in search of our next meal, our ability to make predictions and educated assumptions helped us estimate when the next herd would run by or what time was best for harvesting wild berries. These assumptions were not flawless, as multiple unaccountable factors could interfere with our plans. A storm could keep herds away or the berries could be picked off by wild animals. However, even these uncontrollable factors were not untouchable. With more data points, we were able to better predict the grazing patterns of wild animals or what weather would look like during a hunting day.

Fast forward to where we are today. We are lucky to still have the ability to make predictions and educated assumptions. The uncontrollable factors around us become less and less untouchable when technology and tools make advanced predictions and information becomes more accessible. Before I head out to the office in the morning, I can check what the weather will be, when the train is coming, where my lunch will be, and what time I can expect to go home and squeeze in time for laundry. I can learn anything I want on the internet, and can share knowledge with connections just a few clicks away. We have so much information about everything available to us that, truly, nothing seems impossible anymore.

However, one truth still remains unchanged: everything will never be in our control. And our anxieties loathe this simple truth enough to make us blind to it.

The widely known butterfly effect supports that any small change during the initial state of a system can be the dependent precedent of much larger changes in later states. In other words, every result is the culmination of chain reactions between multiple smaller reactions. One small nudge at any point could have exponential impact later. Simply forgetting to close the window before you head out for the day could cause a draft to blow in and freeze condensation around your heating system so it malfunctions, meaning when you arrive home, you need to endure a cold night before the heater can be fixed the following morning. You wake up sick and unable to get out of bed, so you call your friend you had lunch plans with. She decides to be a good friend and shows up at your door with a fresh-cooked meal she pushed off a first date to prepare, therefore missing her chances with another potential partner who, under a different series of events, would be her future husband.

It would not be wrong to state that your carelessness in forgetting to close the window caused your friend to miss her potential marriage prospect, but most people would agree that linking responsibility to you is a stretch. Yet, our anxieties allow us to do exactly that. We beat ourselves up over choices made in the past that, while perhaps partially responsible for the current result, are not the only factors leading up to it.

While there certainly exist mathematical theorems that help us optimize every little part of our lives, most of us do not carry our days thinking of these. We do not consider probability theorems each time we debate which batch of carrots to pick up at the store, nor do we consider mathematical formulas when we decide to take a different exit on the way home. We make choices using whatever data is currently most available to us and arrive at a point of "good enough"; we may not have the best price or the prettiest batch of carrots in the entire city, but we are content with what we chose. As we stare at carrots in the grocery store, we do not consider theorems supporting which to grab or whether we should change grocery stores altogether. While a silly example, the same can be applied to larger choices like renting a home, buying a car, or choosing a life partner. There is always room for improvement, but we predetermine that searching for such is not worth the effort and are happy with the good enough. We subconsciously make trade-off considerations and believe the effort and work needed to find the best (determined through subjective criteria) does not justify the difference in additional utility and happiness gained.

Something similar can be said when we analyze retrospective anxieties. When we rack our brains and blame ourselves for not making a better choice at an earlier stage, we give ourselves too much confidence in our assumptions. Or, as my therapist would say it, we assume we are perfect in our thinking and know exactly what would happen.

We assume that if we'd left the house just a minute earlier, we could have caught the train and not been ten minutes late to work. However, the butterfly effect would disagree. While it is possible we could have shown up to work on time, it is also very possible that leaving a minute earlier might have meant we left behind an important report, causing us to later have to make an additional trip during lunch to retrieve it. Or perhaps the previous train got caught in a technical accident and was stalled on the tracks for a whole twenty minutes, causing you to be later than if you missed that train altogether. Even if all the choices you make go according to plan, the possibilities of what could have happened are endless.

As long as external factors exist (spoiler alert: they do), then we will never be able to play the godlike hand of knowing exactly how things might have been. Even with the most advanced technologies and the most data points helping us gather information, any room for improvement means there is also room for error. That is just a part of life. We will never fully know everything or have access to all the information that can possibly exist. Nothing ever truly goes according to plan.

It makes no sense to make assumptions with only one data point. How can we make a prediction about what the weather will be two days from now if we are only told the shape of the clouds today? We are interested in also knowing the wind speed, the incoming cold and warm fronts, the time of year, and much more. With just the shape of the clouds today, any prediction about more than the shape of the clouds today is a form of extrapolation. Any sane mathematician can detail the dangers of extrapolation, but it does not take much to understand what they are. By making far-reaching assumptions based on a single data point, noise and other determining factors are not considered and leave much to the imagination about how far off the predictions lie.

At the same time, however, overfitting is a danger to math (and machine learning) as well. When it has too many data points and too many factors to consider, the model becomes too complicated, as any change to any data point of any factor throws predictions in wildly different directions. It becomes nearly impossible to observe trends when every slight variance is a noise-causing incident. In other words, it becomes overwhelmingly complicated to both expect and draw predictions from copious data—so overwhelmingly complicated that its pursuit would be a disappointing and ironic display of human agency.

Expecting the existence of data so copious is impossible. It accounts for every possible external factor so we can make predictions with reliable accuracy.

Last, our anxieties carry a distrust of the "good enoughs" in this world as long as "betters" exist. If there is opportunity to achieve greater and higher expectations, then we believe we should have the means to reach them. How can we settle on the good enoughs when the betters taunt us from every direction? Perhaps this solution is simpler than we think: a reframing of self could be all it takes.

When we give ourselves expectations, we carry an assumption that the expectation is achievable, realistic, and possible. Therefore, our anxieties berate us when we fall short, drowning us in self-effacing thoughts. While easier said than done, perhaps what we need to do is reframe expectations as goals. Unlike expectations, goals are far-reaching and may not be achieved with our current positions and information, but they are still within our horizons. Where do the expectations then go and become?

Nowhere.

Until we are able to let go of our expectations for ourselves, we will never be at peace with the good enoughs of the world. For me, that is much too suffocating a way to live.

Understanding the butterfly effect's prevalence around us should provide even the most anxious with comfort that there is futility in attempting to optimize and perfect everything. This is not a disadvantage to the world but, instead, a conquering of self by learning how to deal with a world of overwhelming knowns and unknowns.

Nothing is impossible in this world, but not everything possible can or should be done. That room in between is the good enough we want to find ourselves in.

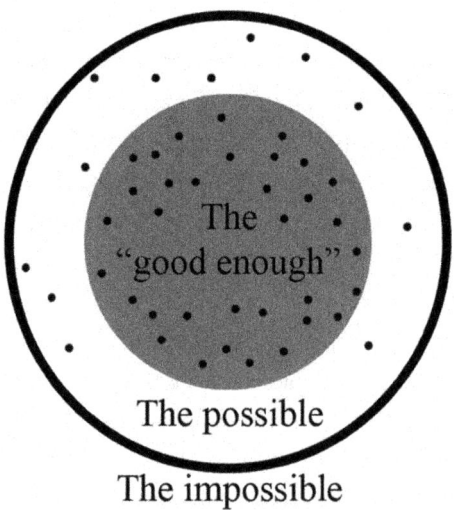

SEPTEMBER 1
PHYSICS

7:32 p.m. Sometimes, when I think about what I've lost in this world, I remember the physics theory that nothing new can ever be created in this world. All the particles are already in existence, and matter cannot be created or destroyed. So I like to think that what I've lost, someone else has gained. And I like to think this someone else needs it more than I do. And if I met that person, maybe we'd be friends. Maybe we'd be more or less than friends, but maybe I'd just be happy they have what used to be mine.

12:44 p.m. We don't ever notice when we're in the right place at the right time but only when we're in the wrong place at the wrong time. There's a lot to be grateful for that we don't think about. **I hope I'm able to spend more time this year focusing on what I haven't been able to appreciate.**

I DO NOT WANT
TO DIE IN MY
SLEEP ONE NIGHT
AND REMEMBER
EVERYTHING I DID
NOT GET TO DO

FEAR OF DEATH

#193: I do not want to die remembering everything I did not get to do.

A common cinematic scene is when a character finds themselves in the last second before their impending death, and their life flashes before their eyes in full HD color with slow-motion montages dragged out with IMAX-theater audio.

Fortunately, we are not movie characters.

Unfortunately, we are still human, and we all die.

I try not to think about every time I came close to death. However, I do try to think about how unbelievably lucky I am to be alive. Perhaps "lucky" is not the best word to use in this case, but it is a marvel that I am alive at all.

Considering the entire universe and the spectrum of time and space, what is the probability that you had a chance of being alive right now, in this place, reading this book? Nearly zero. To start, we need to consider the many events leading up to your life: your parents meeting out of all the people in the world who could have met, your parents deciding to know each other long enough to have a child, your parents having a child (especially in the daunting reality of how many more failed relationships there are than successful ones). Let's not even get into the odds of the exact sperm and the exact egg joining to become you, or the odds of your ancestors producing generations that led to your unbroken lineage. This is too much math for me to even think about.

I am not good at math. But given how many near-death experiences I've landed myself in, I know the chances of me still being alive are negative.

Don't check if that makes sense. I told you I'm not good at math.

I am not a movie character, but each time I came to what I thought would be my last moment in this world, I realized why movies cast the same cinematic scenario over and over again. In those moments, I was overwhelmed by feelings of remorse, guilt, and regret most of all.

The less we live today, the more there is to regret tomorrow.

Every time I woke up in a hospital bed, I thought about everything I regretted. I thought about the people I never got to say thank you to, the activities I never got to do, and everything I'd had to put up with.

I hope you never find yourself in such a position. The regret is overwhelming, paralyzing.

They say the most common deathbed regret is not having done all one wanted to do. Unlike those at their deathbeds, however, I was given another chance—another chance I did not deserve, but another chance, nonetheless.

The first time I found myself in a hospital bed with tubes and unknown machines strapped to me, the regret hit me like an oversized truck speeding on a highway. What came immediately afterward was something I did not expect: conflict.

You would think that after someone is hit with regret the size of an oversized truck, they would do all they could to never feel like that again. They would vow to do all they wanted to do, to live life to the fullest they could. Maybe that is what a rational person would do.

Despite the oversized-regret truck that hit me, I found myself asking a question I did not like: Can I afford to live my life to the fullest now?

The key words here are *afford* and *now*. When we are young, we build up our future and prepare for the next chapter of our lives. We sacrifice social events, enjoyable activities, and leisure time for the promise of a greater chance at a greater future. This kind of lifestyle isn't wrong—we need a roof over our heads and meals on the table—but why is it that so many on their deathbeds do not feel like they were able to live their life to the fullest? Should we not expect that, in the later years of our lives, we would be able to finally reap the harvest we raised?

And that, my friends, is where we overestimate our human abilities.

The desire to save for rainy days and prepare for the unexpected is completely natural. Should it come at the expense of our present joys and happiness? No one can make that choice except you.

Like much (if not everything) in our lives, it comes down to a fine balance. We cannot survive if all we do is enjoy our lives without concern for tomorrow, but we also cannot say we are living if all we do is sacrifice today's happiness for tomorrow. As much as I wish it, an algorithm or mathematical blueprint to best quantify and chart this balance does not exist. It truly is up to each of us to decide how much present happiness we should sacrifice for future gain, and vice versa.

A common fallacy is living our entire lives overcompensating for future gain. Why else do so many regret the way they labored away all their lives? As humans, our brains are miracle machines. They help us sense danger and plan ahead, ensuring we are able to maximize our survival. Society has evolved to support this pursuit and to maintain the well-being of future generations. But when can we stop to think about ourselves?

This conundrum shows itself in multiple tangible applications. The most common are the questions surrounding retirement: When is the perfect time to retire? How much should we save up? Will it be enough to support the lifestyle we want? Maybe, if we work just one more year, we can have a few better days in the future. So we allow ourselves to work one more year. And one more. And one more after that.

Do not be so caught up in making a living for your future that you forget to make a life in your present.

The conflict knotted around me as I lay on my hospital bed was evidence of another human fallacy: taking life for granted. None of us expect ourselves to end up in a hospital bed tomorrow, yet there is also no guarantee telling us we will not. If we are healthy humans with healthy lifestyles, we fairly assume we will not end up in a hospital bed, but no promise ensures our lives will not take a pivot even in a few hours.

Simply asking whether I could afford to live my life to the fullest now was evidence of an assumption: the assumption that I would have a future. Obviously, I do not plan my life like I know when I will die. With that type of clairvoyance, I would be living much differently. Why do we live like we know we will continue to live? Both are predictions and assumptions we have no evidence of yet structure our lives around.

What is the purpose of building up a future we might not be able to live in?

The saying about living like you'll die tomorrow is cliché. Once again, it really comes down to finding a balance that works for each of us. For some, the continuous preparation for the future is fulfilling and meaningful. But to the majority of humans, this is not the case, and this in-between balance is where negotiations must be made.

For the rare, lucky few who are able to save for their future while doing what they love, consider yourselves blessed. You are doing great. You have no need to make negotiations between your future and current selves if both are satisfied with your present-day actions. For the rest of us, such a position feels like a nearly impossible dream. But it is not completely impossible.

This is where we face two choices: we either learn to negotiate, or we change our lives and become those lucky few.

During my most recent hospitalization this year, I had a lot of time to stare at another white ceiling while surrounded by my regrets. After all these years and emergency room terrors, I was still taking life for granted and telling myself I could not afford to live now. How many times would finally scare me out of being scared of living?

While I am still in the midst of figuring out this balance for myself, I found two practices I do every day to alleviate the regrets. First, I spend time every day sharing daily gratitude with the people close to me. I like to write down and reflect on my day and think about all I was grateful for and all I was happy I experienced. Thinking only of the absence of good in life can be all too easy. This practice allows me to spend more time each day being aware of when I feel happy. From the smallest moments ("Wow, I got an extra chicken nugget!") to the biggest ones ("My best friend announced she's coming back to town!"), filling my life with appreciation helps me take life less for granted and more with gratitude.

Second, I ask myself every night how I would feel if I wasn't going to wake up in the morning. When I look back on a life I can no longer change, will I feel fulfilled? So much has happened in my past that I cannot change, and I have come to peace with those things in their own ways (making peace with some of them is still in progress). But I do not want to focus on what was too far in the past and what I can no longer touch. Instead, I want to focus on the day itself. If I were to not wake up tomorrow morning, would I feel satisfied with the life I led today? From preparations for a future safety net to moments of letting myself be present in my happiness, was it a good day? After days, weeks, and months of asking myself this question, the answers build up to one for a greater question: Did I have a good life?

The flowers make up the garden. We need to start tending each flower before we can see the garden bloom.

Perhaps this is why I no longer have a fear of death. I have a fear of how I may die (I am quite the softie and cannot handle pain), but I am no longer scared of death itself. When it comes, I hope to welcome its arrival knowing I lived as fulfilling a life as I could in this world. I no longer want to be fearful of the day I leave.

"What would you do if you only had a year left to live?" Answers I often receive include, "I would tell my friends how much I love them and how much I appreciate them," "I would quit my job and go boating all year," and "I would spend the rest of my time spending all the money I've earned and eating good food." These answers bring out what we truly want in our lives, what we believe we are aiming the future toward. Unfortunately, we will never be asked that question other than in the hypothetical sense. We will never know when we are down to our last year in this world. When do we start living and stop merely making a living?

You have two choices. And you can start anytime you like.

JULY 9
POETRY

Thinking about the lowest point of today made me think about the poem I wrote as a freshman for the open mic night our dorm put on during the first week of school. I look back at her—freshman Emily—and I so often wish I was still her. I was wide-eyed, eager to make friends, and unaware of the troubles the rest of my college years would bring me. She was a girl who, though she wished to be prettier and skinnier, was also confident and happy in her body. I miss her. She didn't know she would break a loved one's heart, be anorexic, have her heart broken, and lose the will to live again like she did four years ago. I wonder what she would have thought if she knew. She was enjoying herself, making new connections with people she didn't know would end up being some of her most loved friends. She was excited to take on the world and see what she could do when she kept moving forward. **I wonder where she went. I hope she's happy now.**

That poem was one of my greatest prides. It's hard that I cannot even remember the title anymore. It was about not having a home anymore but finding a new home in oneself. "Today I ran away from the sky, not because I was running away from it, but because I know I will remember it." Those aren't the exact words, I know, but it's a fragment of my favorite line.

Maybe I should get back into poetry. I forgot when and why I stopped writing.

IT IS OKAY TO LET
IT HURT BUT
REMEMBER TO
ALSO LET IT HEAL
AND THEN LET IT
GO FOR GOOD

THERAPY

#10: It is okay to let it hurt but remember to also let it heal and then let it go for good.

Do I recommend therapy for everyone? Yes and no.

The first time I interacted with therapy, I absolutely loathed the experience. While I had sessions of group therapy and individual therapy during my time in the mental hospital, I knew the care I received would not be long-term and was used more as a proxy to decide when I could be discharged. When I left the hospital, I started state-mandated therapy sessions. Since I was a minor at the time, my parents were present. Obviously, no child who was in a mental hospital because of how suffocated she felt at her own house would be willing to say much during these sessions. Paired with parents who did not believe in the validity of mental illness, every session went a bit like this:

"Hi Emily. I hear you've had a handful of suicide attempts?"
"Yeah."
"What kinds of thoughts led to these attempts?"
"I just really hate myself."
"Really? What is going on that makes you feel this way?"

"She's completely fine. It's probably just a phase, you know teenagers and how moody they are. She has a lot to be grateful for. She's always top of class and has lots of friends in school. This is just her being dramatic."

"Thank you for your input, ma'am, but this is time for Emily to answer."

"Sure."

My memories of those sessions are vague and hazy, perhaps because I was half-asleep more than I was awake.

The next interaction I had with therapy was in college when I was going through my anorexia. I did not have insurance, so I was only able to attend a limited number of sessions the college provided. The sessions felt useless, which was likely a product of knowing I would not be seeing the therapist long-term mixed with my distrust of school therapists (I was wary of any potential ulterior motives). Another data point was added to my not-so-great experiences with therapy.

By the time I was nearing graduation, I stopped giving therapy a chance. Many people in my life suggested I try therapy, but each time I rebuffed them, saying I already had and it was not for me. I wasn't lying. I liked to think I spent more time in my head than the average person. Having already read extensive literature on my mental disorders, I also believed I was much more self-aware than the average person. I did pick up a few therapy sessions here and there, never sticking with a therapist for long. I either felt I wasn't learning anything new or got frustrated with how I was siloed into a teenage-angst stereotype and not listened to. Therapists frequently paused sessions and asked how I felt, to which I responded nonchalantly, "Indifferent, really. I already had this conversation in my head." Having had these disorders all my life, I had already spent hours and hours in constant debate with myself, exploring new perspectives and trying to think of new framings.

I used to tell people therapy was not for me because I already knew what I needed to do to help myself. Some therapists in the middle provided me with tactical actions and direction, which I found insightful and useful. Therapists provide patients with guidance, but ultimately, it is up to the patient to make the next steps. You can bring a horse to water, but you cannot make it drink—much like how therapists can equip a patient with all the knowledge they have, but their patient must apply it to their own life however they see fit. Because I kept reaching a point with therapists where I became frustrated at how little new insight I was gaining, I decided what I needed was no longer therapy. I needed to put into action the directions I was left with.

I was neither right nor wrong. Why? Simply because it all comes down to how we approach therapy and what we are looking to get out of it.

A small voice in the back of my head always hoped therapy could help me. I did not want to give up on therapy for myself, yet it never felt like I wished it would. I jumped from periods of attending therapy to dry spells without. Near the end of an extremely rough year, I was seeing three therapists at the same time, all for different problems I was dealing with. As I developed relationships with each of them, I began to learn what was working well for me and what was not, and most importantly, what I wanted out of therapy sessions. Now, I am down to one therapist whom I see multiple times during the week. And I do not intend on stopping anytime soon.

I am not a certified expert telling people they need therapy or how to find the right therapist. That is a process I myself am still learning. However, through my complicated relationship with therapy, I did learn a thing or two that I hope can support your journey to seek help.

1. **Know what you are looking for in therapy, and look for it.** A friend who recently began therapy told me they did not feel they were getting what they were looking for out of it. I asked them what they wanted out of therapy, and they responded, "Well, that's what I'm still figuring out." This was not the first time I received that answer when someone told me they were unsure why they decided to begin therapy. And it is completely okay. Perhaps you are in therapy to simply figure out if you need therapy. Well, there is no better way than to experience it. You do not know what you need until you need it for the first time, and a therapist could help you figure out if there is something you want to work on.

   The same can be said for individuals seeking therapy for very specific reasons. Do some light reading before you start to understand what kind of therapist you need, what kind of treatment you will need, and anything else that can help you shape who an ideal therapist will be. Read up on the backgrounds of the therapists you have test sessions with to insure they list experience matching what you are looking for. Once you start developing a rapport with them, communicate to them why you are in therapy and what your goals are, even if those goals are simply to figure out what you are looking to get out of therapy.

2. **One session may not be enough.** I do not know about you, but there is absolutely not enough time to both let my therapist know everything that goes on in one week and have a fruitful conversation regarding my feelings

about all of it. At one point, I was having sessions nearly every day because of all the change happening in my daily life. As you reach the end of a really good session, ask the therapist if they have an opening coming up so you can pick up the conversation. Trust me: they appreciate when you add another session on the calendar rather than trying to rush through a week's worth of events in a limited time.

3. **Therapy is meaningless without transparency.**
They say when the rose-colored glasses come off, the red flags finally become red flags. If your therapist is helping you to remove the rose-colored tint from your glasses, do not just close your eyes until they are done. Therapy is a conversation. If you are unable to be fully honest and transparent with your therapist about the thoughts going on in your head, then they do not have anything to work on with you. It understandably does and should take time for each of us to grow comfortable enough with an individual, so do not be let down if the rose-colored tint is still on your glasses after the first trial. However, when I found myself still unable to say certain things to my therapist after a few months into our sessions, I decided I needed to find a different therapist who I felt safer chatting with.

While I still frequently say to my therapist, "I feel indifferent about our conversation because I already had this conversation in my head," I am making a greater effort to be open-minded about the new perspectives our conversations invite. As much as I like to think I think a lot, there are always new pieces of insight to be observed and discussed.

Be in tune with yourself when going into therapy. If your therapist says something that frustrates you, you should express that. Talking about therapy in therapy is okay. You should have open discussions with your therapist about what has and has not been working for you. When it comes to taking care of yourself, you need to put yourself first.

4. **Therapy is for you.** Your therapist is not you. Your therapist cannot and will not fix your problems for you. Only you will be able to heal yourself, and your therapist is simply another individual who can help you get there. However, you cannot become reliant on your therapist and expect them to have a key that unlocks all of your solutions. This means when entering therapy sessions, if you bring in anything less than your full presence and attention, you cannot expect to get the most out of your therapist. It means scheduling your sessions at times you will not forget when you will not be easily distracted. It means knowing what you want to discuss with your therapist. It means leaving room to be taught something new, even if you do not ultimately agree with it.

I spend the days before therapy keeping small notes on what I want to talk about during the session so we have content instead of rambling and seeing where things go. After sessions, I make sure to spend at least ten minutes reflecting on what we discussed, writing down any notes for the following week that I want to keep in mind. Whether you take in what your therapist says is up to you. They may provide useful insight, but if you simply leave what is discussed within the session, then you are not applying it to the rest of your life where it should be shared. Effective therapy happens when the patient and the therapist work together, not on a one-way street.

5. **Not every therapist is for you.** Looking for a therapist is like dating. The first one you chat with will not always be the best match, but the one you did not expect can be the perfect one for you. Develop a system for yourself that will help you decide whether or not you continue with a therapist. Each of us looks for something different in a therapist, much like how we look for different traits in our partners. Maybe you prefer a therapist that does more talking than you, or you prefer one who will ask questions and let you ramble. Maybe you want one that makes you feel comfortable and at home, or maybe you prefer a therapist that keeps you thinking on your feet. Spend some time understanding who will work best with you and what those sessions should ideally look like. If you decide to end your sessions, there are no hard feelings. Therapists understand, and they want you to find the best fit for your needs.

Everyone can benefit from therapy. It truly is just heart-to-heart conversation between two individuals in a vulnerable space designed to support healing processes. However, like anything else in our lives, doing it for the sake of doing it (like attending state-mandated sessions with little to no interest) will never result in the solutions you hope for. Your therapists have therapists, too, and all of them are humans like you. Their job is to support their patients, so the least you can do is help them help you.

JULY 8

9:05 p.m. I was reminded again today that I need therapy. Therapy is too expensive and a cost I cannot take on at the moment given what has happened recently, but I need to try.

You were the second friend to offer to pay for my therapy. When you offered to help, it made me realize again that if you believe therapy would be so important for me that you would be willing to support me, then the least I can do to repay you is to try.

JULY 13

10:54 p.m.

*I questioned myself a lot today. **I realized I need therapy.** I not only needed it in the past, but now I need therapy because of this breakup. This breakup made me question myself and my validity. It brought to the surface how my happiness has always relied on others, and I was always making myself happy by making others happy. But this breakup broke me as well. It made me question my depression and whether or not it was real. It made me ask myself if I truly was depressed, or if I was simply seeking attention all these years of my life. The more I questioned, the more I couldn't help but beat myself more and more into a dark corner. When I was speaking to you, and when I said I could no longer tell if I was ever suicidal or depressed or just whiny, I realized how desperate this breakup made me for my identity. It made me question a part of me I never questioned since high school. To have to ask myself such core and integral questions helped me see that I am no longer okay.*

11:21 p.m. Today at therapy, he told me about how therapy really works. I come to him to explain my experiences, and he explains to me how my experiences make me think. It's funny to think this is how simple it really is. But it really does work. It's the ability to have someone validate and explain to you the emotions you feel are real. It's being told what you feel is legitimate and there is a reason, controlled by your past experiences, why you feel the way you do. That's really all there is.

JULY 24
ENDINGS

When does therapy end? When do you know you are fully healed and recovered and ready to take on the world? Do we ever truly reach that point, or is it just something we tell ourselves? I don't believe I'll ever be completely healed and recovered to how I used to be. I don't think there's anything wrong with that, either. But I also believe the true tests come when we are in another darker, lower place. It's easy to say recovery is going smoothly and well when we aren't experiencing extremely heavy emotions. How will we be able to know we are stronger if we are not tested? How will I ever know therapy is enough and that my healing journey is over? What if I end up needing more care—more than therapy can provide?

OUR DAYS ARE
NOT MEASURED BY
DEGREES OF
PRODUCTIVITY
BUT BY DEGREES
OF PRESENCE

PRODUCTIVITY

#332: Our days are not measured by degrees of productivity but by degrees of presence.

Humankind's progression in technology and society opened doors to wondrous possibilities for everyone. Opportunities abound. The world is a big, beautiful place for the starry-eyed, curious adventurer.

On the other hand, the world is also an absolutely paralyzing and exhausting place for the workaholic.

It goes without saying that hustle culture has exploded during our time. As each generation replaces the one before, we are pushed to test our limits, exploring the world in every nook and cranny. We grow competitive and fierce as we strive to be the best versions of ourselves. Young children accomplish feats and overcome challenges impossible for the wisest of adults just 100 years earlier. We no longer worry about where we will have our next meal and instead can spend our thinking on inventing the next hottest start-up. Truly, the world has become an amazing place.

For some of us, however, this level of advancement makes us obsessed with productivity. We are addicted to always getting work done, pushing ourselves to inhumane levels just to get in another hour. Especially growing up in the Bay Area where competition was intense from a young age, my community ingrained in me the reality that there was always someone better or working harder than me. Therefore, there was no excuse to not be working even harder. Soon enough, this became a part of my identity.

My friends often characterize me as a workaholic. I do not have a moment in my day when I am not thinking about how to maximize my productivity or how to optimize my waking hours. Typically, I get roughly six hours of sleep before leaping out of bed and spending the rest of my eighteen hours working through a packed calendar, in which my day is planned down to the thirty-minute interval. As a college student, I juggled board positions, three part-time restaurant jobs an hour's commute away, additional classes to graduate early, a freelance business, multiple internships, and social life. Typing up homework assignments while riding the train home at midnight after a shift and simultaneously planning when to wake up the next morning to make a call was common for me. It felt exhilarating when my whole day passed by as I crossed tasks off my checklist and made my way down my calendar, all according to my meticulously planned schedule.

I was told I am "motivating" and an "inspiration to work harder" by starry-eyed, curious underclassmen. They asked what keeps me going and working so hard. To be honest, my inability to answer this question is what plagues me to this day.

When my peers tell me they could never be like me, a "working machine," I tell them I am happy for them. I do not wish anyone to be like me.

My inability to put down my work is a problem, not a blessing.

Unfortunately, I know many others like me exist, struggling on a day-to-day basis to understand why they work so hard. Working this hard is almost a blessing and a curse. Instead of fearing how we will keep a roof over our heads, we fear not having enough work to keep us busy.

For us, putting down our work to have rest, a mental break, or playtime seems absolutely absurd. Why should we rest if we can be productive? It feels counterintuitive. As a college student, I gave up every single weekend to work at restaurants, filling my days with double shifts Friday to Sunday and working from 10:00 a.m. to midnight. I never let myself miss a shift of work to attend social gatherings or any other form of leisurely enjoyment. If I did, I beat myself up later, calculating the opportunity cost of how much money I could earn had I taken my usual shift.

These thoughts cursed me for years. Rather than enjoy time with my friends, I counted how much money I lost by not being at work. Regardless of how much homework or client work I took on, I always accepted more projects and shifts. My motto was that I had enough faith in myself that some way, somehow, I would find a way to fit it all into my day. This compromised my health. Meals were skipped or sleep was scrapped.

When freshmen "wanted to know how I did it," I told them the key to time and work management was, if everything truly mattered enough to them, they would find the way to make everything fit into their schedule. It made sense to me that one would prioritize the most important activities and make sure they could all be accomplished, even at the expense of the lesser important ones. I had no problem giving up break or mealtimes if it meant I could squeeze in more work.

More than anything, I felt responsible for everything touching my life. Despite my friends and loved ones repeatedly telling me there are many factors in my life I cannot control, I always founds ways to point all catastrophes back to mistakes I made. My philosophy was that I had more control over the outcomes in my life than I wanted to believe. If I missed a question on a test, then I blamed myself for not studying enough the night before because I had to quickly finish up a client project, which I pushed off since I forgot to complete a homework assignment on my train ride home from work the night before that. I never forgave myself for any mistake. I could always do better, so I needed to push myself more.

This was a vicious cycle. My high-functioning depression and anxiety diagnosis meant I could perform well to the point that it was difficult to see I was suffering from mental disorders. When I did fall into a darker place, I fell quickly and with intense mood swings. Similarly, I bounced back very quickly, often returning to work within an hour. During these moments, I told myself I did not have time to break down, and I beat myself up for wasting time being anxious. Just keep going, I would tell myself.

As proud as I was for my accomplishments, I was also exhausted from living. When I went on dates with my boyfriend, I found myself feeling guilty for wishing I was at work instead, but it was a feeling I could not shake off. Eventually, I became convinced that I was just slower than most other people, so I needed to be harder on myself and work more than them.

Every moment I rested was a moment I could get work done. No breaks.

My working schedule and to-do list never ended. When asked if I ever took a break, I said my breaks were the occasional bus commutes or slower times at restaurant shifts when I chatted with coworkers. I was content with these "breaks" scattered in my day.

I was also constantly guilty of comparing myself to others. It looked like others were far more successful than me in places where I dedicated countless hours. I surmised the reasoning must simply be they were smarter or more efficient than me, so it was my fault alone. I needed to spend more time to reach half of their level. It never occurred to me how strange it was that I worked more than anyone else I knew.

No matter how my friends reasoned with me, nothing they said made sense. What was most important to me was advancing myself and earning as much money as I could to save up for rainy days. That was how I'd been taught since I was a young child.

Over time, this resulted in consequences that slowly bled into various parts of my life. I developed migraines at the age of twenty, forcing me to frequently sit down and shut my eyes tight to gain balance over my spinning world. Twice a week at restaurant shifts I felt like I was on the brink of collapse. My social life began to suffer, as I did not dedicate time to friends. My anorexia partially stemmed from believing it logically made no sense for me to waste time eating, so I cut down on mealtimes until they were completely dismissed from my schedule. Needless to say, I was more than obsessed with working. And I could not break free of it.

One of my clearest memories of my mother is from a day in high school. She sat me down and told me she was sorry I took after my father, who was obsessed with working. He never seemed happy when I was a child, always complaining that there was so much to be done. His sense of responsibility did not let him leave tasks for others to pick up. At the time,

I pitied him. He was the sole source of income for my family and had the duty of keeping a roof over our heads. I watched him lie on the couch after work every day, exhausted and caught in a repeating cycle.

I was only twenty years old and already putting myself through the same thing.

Regardless of what age you are, being caught in this vicious cycle is absolutely devastating. It drains the life from you. It bleeds you slowly. You feel like you cannot leave because more can always be done. After all, isn't this what everyone else around you is doing? Hustle harder, right?

Sit down for a moment, please. I know breaking away from this massive rat race pushes you from every angle. I have just one question for any of you who felt an unsettling ring in your heart as you read this chapter and found yourself looking at your own reflection: Are you living to be happy?

I never let myself compromise any of my work or productivity to pursue happiness. I could achieve happiness later in life. I could chase that elusive dream of happiness when I was in a more stable place after I finished hustling. My younger years were meant for working hard so my later years could be spent in leisure, right? Never mind the social gatherings, birthday parties, or weekend celebrations. I did not need those. They made me feel carefree and full of life in the moment but did not contribute toward my success. All I needed was work.

Could I have let myself consider that cultivating happiness and well-being is a form of productivity?

Maybe a better question is: Are you defining your worth through your productivity?

It took me too many years to learn this, too many years to realize the weekends I spent with friends, the parties where I danced the night away, and the celebrations where I laughed until I cried were all productive toward being the best I could be. Our well-being, both mentally and physically, needs to be nourished for us to live.

I believe productivity is not just measured by the number of hours spent with your nose in a book. It's not just the number in your bank account or the accolades you accumulate for a résumé. Productivity is making memories with people who make you happy you decided to come out tonight, and photos filled with cherished smiles you will look at when you are eighty years old.

Productivity is every single passing second you are still in this world, every morning you still wake up to, every hill you climb, and every moment you celebrate. This lesson is difficult to learn, but do not let life pass you by.

A commonly heard regret of people on their deathbeds is that they did not live when they had the opportunity to do so. I did not need to be on my deathbed to feel the weight of regret absorb me. I watched my friends make memories without me, watched them laugh together about inside jokes I thought were unnecessary compared to the work I was producing. Despite the isolation and exhaustion I felt, I kept telling myself I was pushing for a better future. Everything I gave up now was a sacrifice for my future self to have a better life. Present me was watching out for future me.

Yet, I still felt twists in my stomach as I watched every missed moment of happiness walk by me. I wished to pursue so many of the dreams that would make me happy in the moment, but I did not let myself. It felt indulgent.

Happiness is not an indulgence. Happiness is productive.

We work diligently in our societies to keep up with advancement. We idolize productivity and success, defining our own self-worth through accomplishments and how elastic we make our own limits. We define our success based on how much work we are able to crank out of our bodies and, in turn, how much worldly satisfaction we achieve.

I can tell myself that I am working hard and sacrificing my well-being so my future self will be happy. Does your future self want that for your present self, though? Does your future self want you to miss out on all the instances you could be laughing and smiling? Your future self knows you work hard, you do not give up, and you will always find opportunities when you need to. This will never change. However, time does not stop for anyone. The moments when you could be laughing and enjoying yourself do not ever repeat again. The happiness you give up now will not be the same happiness you can experience later. Each moment of happiness we can reach is precious. We will always have time to work harder, but each memory only has one chance.

In this world, we measure productivity by our successes, but success is so much more than a job title or numbers in your retirement account. Reframe how you view success and what you count as an achievement. Celebrate more and recognize yourself for your hard work. Maybe you do not need to pack your schedule back-to-back to optimize how much you can get done. Success might be having a day when you are able to enjoy yourself without typing away at a computer like you always thought you needed to. Achievements are sweeter when you learn to celebrate the smaller ones too. Maybe success is simply trying when we do not want to be trying. Maybe we are successful right now, more than we think we are.

Maybe future you wants present you to take a break and be proud of yourself.

You might be most productive right now if you stop what you are doing. Stopping yourself before burning out means you will be able to perform at a regular, steady pace instead of working in choppy, irregular, and unreliable jerks. We cannot force ourselves to continue working when we are running on our last drops of fuel and then expect the same level of output. If we go for an extended run, we know we need water to keep our bodies going. Similarly, we need mental breaks to keep our hearts going. Being productive means not just knowing when to rest but when to stop completely. Maybe stopping early is what you need.

One day, you may realize that happiness means being kind to yourself and listening to your heart. It means learning how to live so you go to bed with a content smile instead of anxieties over everything you could and should do.

In this life, we can be productive whenever we want. Our society has blessed us with so many resources and opportunities everywhere, even when we are not searching. We will never miss out on work. We will always have work when we want to work. Yet, we will miss out on the life we do not live.

Your life and your success are about you. Success was never meant to be about who could be the best or who was able to be more productive. You are productive when you wake up and live. You are growing yourself and advancing yourself through every experience you have, through every moment you live and learn. It does not matter to your happiness if someone else has a bigger salary than you. You are not them. You will not lose money because of their gain. It does not matter to your happiness if someone else is better than you at a subject you always underperformed in. You are not them, and you are better than them at something else you may not realize. Regardless, your happiness is not reliant on the status or well-being of others but on yourself.

Future you wants you to know they are proud of you. No one compares to you except your past self. You do not live the lives of others, so what purpose is there in comparing your experiences and related consequences with theirs? That is no way to live. Do not live your life through the lens of others' lives. Live your life by looking through your own lens by comparing your present self with your past self. Learn to love and cherish present self so that future self has a stronger, happier foundation to start on.

Make yourself laugh. Make yourself smile. You are doing great, and you always will be. Take a breath and keep going. This is your life to live and enjoy.

AUGUST 15

11:23 p.m. This past week I felt incredibly unproductive, like I had done nothing that would further my career or academic paths. I know if this had occurred to me earlier during the stay-at-home, I would be beating myself up more than I am right now. I feel like this quarantine has helped me learn the importance of giving myself a break when I'm used to running at 300 mph every day. It taught me to prioritize and focus on my mental health, and I know while I may not be working or being productive in my traditional definition, the steps I've made to improve my mental health this season will be what I am most proud of. I hope one day I will be able to see my work for my mental health as productivity as well. I think it shows I still have a ways to go to accept this myself.

11:34 p.m. Searching for happiness is such a privilege.

I think I'm slowly understanding that happiness can only be defined in the moment. It doesn't matter what has happened in our past or what may happen in our future. Happiness is defined by what we feel at this very moment.

It's hard for us to let go of the past, to detach our past efforts and failures from our happiness in the moment. Even if we feel like we are enjoying ourselves in the moment, we still look back at our past—at what we have done and all we regret—and wonder if we are truly happy. But if we are happy in the present, then that's all there is—isn't it?

But it's such a privilege to be able to search for happiness.

Anyone at any point in their life can realize what happiness is. They can realize what happiness means for them and what the little moments are that define what happiness feels like for them. However, the ability to search for the means to maximize that happiness is a privilege. Only those who feel they are safe, stable, and have their survival needs met have the capacity to search for their happiness. I can't help but wonder if I am truly in this place.

I think there's also happiness in being self-aware, or at least self-aware enough to know I am not yet at a point of having the capability to search for my happiness. But I do know what that happiness means and looks like. I know right now I am still in phases of struggling and recovery that may not always be linear. But I know I am now aware of what happiness looks like. And when I am able to, I will not waste time. I will achieve it.

DO IT FOR THE
FRIENDS YOU
HAVE NOT MET

FRIENDS

#228: Do it for the friends you have not met.

When I am not doing the best mentally, it can be incredibly difficult for my friends to support me. At times, I just want to be alone and shut down, isolated from everyone. Other times, I do not trust that I will not be judged for the meltdowns I have. And at other times, I feel like I am a burden to the friends I do turn to, especially if they are too nice to turn me away and end up in a position to comfort me when they did not want to. No matter the reason, it stops my friends from supporting me.

If you have ever been on the opposite end of this, then you know how frustrating and worrisome it is when someone you care about is unable to communicate their needs to you. You want to help them and genuinely, wholeheartedly support them, but they are not receptive for various reasons.

Neither friend is at fault. Oftentimes, communication during tense, urgent situations is just difficult. This is why it is necessary for healthy friendships and habits to develop before the moments of tension. Every friendship looks different, and these practices helped me find greater trust and support in my friends.

JOURNAL

For those of us who have a hard time expressing emotions and thoughts to someone else, we find it easier to write them down. Writing also helps cleanse the mind, forcing us to put our nebulous thoughts into concrete language. When I begin writing to someone about my day, I write for a long time without stopping. One thought leads to another, producing messages I would likely not be able to verbally express. By keeping a shared journal between you and your friends, you can communicate emotions and events that may not be easily shared verbally. A journal makes its writers feel more vulnerable and open, oftentimes drawing out deeply personal thoughts they might have felt trouble expressing outside of writing. This is especially helpful if you or your friends have life circumstances making it difficult to regularly chat.

CHECK IN

It warms my heart greatly when I am in the middle of a busy day and am unable to really speak with anyone, yet out of the blue, a friend checks in on me. It feels like, "Wow! I meant enough to this person that, without prompting, they decided to reach out to me." My friends and I check in on each other at least once a week. When someone checks in on you, you need to let them know how you are doing in that moment. No barriers—just let it all out. A friend I had not spoken to in a year once messaged me, and I told him something along the lines of, "I had a breakdown, I am overwhelmed, but I want to sleep. How about you?" Rather than deal with small talk, diving straight into asking how someone's emotional state has been that day opens up a channel for vulnerability. You need to let your friends check on you to see how you are. This is different from a usual "How are you doing?" because it shows a friend's focus on you. They had enough time to ask if you were doing okay. And they chose to do that.

ASK WHAT THEY NEED

When your friend is not doing well or wants to get something off their chest, always ask what they want from you. Are they looking for advice, or just a shoulder to cry on? Are they looking for someone who listens or someone who responds after every pause? Each person has different preferences, and each person's preferences change from situation to situation. These preferences are not offensive but helpful. For example, it becomes frustrating when I vent to a friend and receive unsolicited advice. Prior to a friend coming to you to talk about anything, ask what they need from you and how that should be best delivered. Furthermore, do not assume just because they had a set of preference the last three times they reached out to you that what worked last time will work this time. Things rarely ever go as planned.

SHARE YOUR GOOD NEWS

I keep a "Good News Update" habit with some of my closest friends. At the end of every night before we head to bed, we tell each other what the good news of the day was. This helps us stay positive by ending our day thinking about the good, and it also helps keep our attitudes optimistic in everyday living. Even if the day felt like it went horribly wrong, the good news at the end of the night can simply be, "At least I am here to tell you goodnight." If we look hard enough, good news is always there.

SAFE WORD

By far, this tip has helped my friendships the most. As much as I want to help a friend who needs someone to talk to or someone to listen, sometimes there is just too much going on in my own life for me to be able to offer that kind of help. I may not be in the best place myself, but I do genuinely want to support them. However, we cannot take care of others before we take care of ourselves. If you find yourself to be similar in this regard, then it is absolutely necessary you take care of yourself before helping others. As a result, there are situations when a friend reaches out to me to talk, and I am humbled to be the person they want to have a vulnerable conversation with. Unfortunately, when I need to take care of myself, it would help no one if we found ourselves in a blind-leading-the-blind interaction to support each other when neither of us were capable at the moment.

If you are familiar with this situation, then you are familiar with being forced to choose between yourself or your friend. To solve this, my friends and I developed a safe word. If one of us is ever in a position of needing emotional support and reaches out to someone, the others can use the safe word (or phrase) to gently let the individual know they would love to help but are unable to at the time. Some individuals worry that using the safe word will be offensive to the one seeking help. Are you not essentially turning away a friend in need when they seek help from you? While this may be true, it would be unhealthy for everyone if you decided to support them despite being unable to support yourself. When the safe word is mentioned, the answering individual no longer needs to explain their situation. With the safe word, they are expressing that while they wish they could help, they are in a position of being unable to. The implementation of this kind of habit in your friendships will allow people to build boundaries for themselves around what they can and cannot offer without sacrificing their own well-being to be there for other friends.

Maybe it's time to check in on a friend and see how they are—isn't it?

DO YOUR BEST TO
BE KIND TO
SOMEONE
EVERYDAY BUT DO
NOT FORGET
THAT YOU ARE A
SOMEONE TOO

ACTS OF KINDNESS

#13: Do your best to be kind to someone every day but do not forget that you are also a someone.

"Don't make eye contact with him," my mom whispered to ten-year-old me in Mandarin on the midafternoon train. "He" was a stranger with baggy clothing, a torn jacket, trampled shoes, and a recycled fountain soda cup with change.

Twenty-year-old me found a stranger with baggy clothing, a torn jacket, trampled shoes, and a recycled fountain soda cup with change on the 1:00 a.m. train. Ten-years-later me handed him my leftovers from the restaurant where I had just finished a shift and a crumpled five-dollar bill. "Sorry, they're kind of cold."

We cannot blame how we are programmed. Just last week, I watched a video of a bewildered husky cautiously approaching a kitten for the first time, completely baffled by the creature it had never seen. Despite the kitten's tiny size compared to the grown husky, the dog was still cautious, slowly sniffing to diagnose and observe as much as it could. Eventually, when it realized the kitten was more friend than foe, it took a careful step forward and licked the newborn, and furry friends were made.

We are not huskies. But we are programmed to be wary of what we do not know.

I was raised to be careful of strangers. I was told to never approach people with tattoos, people who drank, people who were loud, people who were "of the wrong crowd." I was raised to be careful of those different from what my parents were used to. However, they were not just "different"; they were the "wrong crowd." We stay away from the "wrong crowd" and defend our family, the "right crowd."

I lose count of the number of times my parents yelled at me in public when I did not come to their defense. When I defended the cashier just trying to do their job, when I defended the server who made a mistake, or when I simply mentioned that maybe, just maybe, we were not always the ones in the right, I received an earful about how I "never defend the right people."

At least, that was how I was supposed to be raised. That was how we are supposed to run.

We are careful of strangers. They are different from us. We do not know their stories the way we know the stories of our friends and family. Profiling strangers from first impressions and then developing our attitudes toward them from there is so, so easy.

While we can call out this harmful behavior, it brings forward a conversation from the other end of the table: How do we keep ourselves safe with limited information? The safer choice is to stay away from strangers we do not know, since we do not know if they have ill intent toward us. Even if they seem like nice folks, we cannot trust them so easily, right? I mean, that is the entire logic behind "don't get into the van of someone who offers you candy."

Man, the world is such a broken place. We can't trust one another anymore. "Guilty until proven innocent" is how we were raised to approach the rest of the world. Yet, at the same time, is there really any alternative that will keep us as safe as possible? The news headlines every day only continue the narrative of what a messed-up world we're in.

As much as I would like to, I cannot paint myself like some divine being sent down from the heavens, declared exempt from human cynicism. In fact, I am probably one of the most cynical people I know.

Like any other small ten-year-old on a train, I was taught yet another life lesson of "do not interact with strangers because that is how you put yourself in danger." I was instructed about what a stranger looked like, but more importantly, I was instructed about what bad strangers, *really* bad strangers, and really, *really* bad strangers look like.

Look like.

As humans, we like repetition and familiarity. If we lived our entire lives following a set of rules and nothing disproved them, we'd see no harm in continuing to live by that set of rules. If we lived our entire lives following a set of rules about who we can be nice to and who we should never make eye contact with, it would make sense to continue if they were not disproven.

We do not really even give ourselves chances to disprove those rules when we give the world a "guilty until proven innocent" outlook, do we?

That is up to each of us to decide. Some of us may be completely fine with knowing we will, statistically speaking, be much less likely to get hurt if we minimize interactions with people who are different. The fewer people we interact with in general, the less opportunity there is to be hurt by others.

Yet for some of us, this cynical way of living just does not feel right.

As humans, we like repetition and familiarity. However, the entire world does not run on the repetition and familiarity we like (that's what makes life fun, isn't it?). When those sets of rules we live within are disproven, we readjust, realign, and redirect our lives to make sure the new rules now include the exception.

How are those rules broken? We give them the opportunity to be broken. We take leaps of faith.

Even the most risk-loving person in the world knows limits. We decide whether a risk is worth taking by weighing its chances against its outcomes. Even if we would like it to be, not everything can be perfectly quantified and deduced in rational terms to see if one end of a ratio outweighs the other. That is what a leap of faith is: a leap forward toward a risk we believe in and find worth hopping for, even if we cannot rationalize its outcomes yet.

Not every leap of faith comes by choice. Sometimes, we do not even realize we are already on the other side of that leap until we look back.

During my time in the mental hospital, the rest of the patients I spent my days with were completely the wrong crowd. They were the ones ten-year-old me on a midafternoon train was told to not make eye contact with. My first day with them, I was running on instinct (I mean, if you were also plucked out of your suburban home and woke up in a mental hospital, you would be careful as well) and sat as far as I could, making as little eye contact as possible. I wanted nothing to do with the wrong crowd. Yet, as the days passed and the other patients became my companions, confidants, and friends, the rules I was raised with were revisited. As I made friends out of the patients, each rule was broken one by one. As I got to know each of their stories, I found the wrong crowd was actually my crowd. I never felt more okay to laugh and be myself than with these individuals who, had we met outside of the hospital, I would have passed by.

My rules were not just broken during my stay. They were completely bent out of shape until they could no longer be rules and started to look a bit more like prejudice. I was shown kindness by people I never gave myself the chance to be kind to.

I am not trying to say I was suddenly reborn into the most kind and open-hearted person this world has ever been blessed to see. I do not think I will get anywhere close to that in my lifetime. What I can say, however, is I am so happy I am now on the other side of that leap of faith.

Obviously, I still live with rules in my life. I'm still human. But maybe now I live with a few less rules and a few more leaps of faith.

Because strangers who did not know my story treated me with kindness, I want to treat strangers whose stories I do not know with the same kindness.

Many called me "naive," "lacking a sense of danger," or straight up "asking to be killed" when I was on the 1:00 a.m. train and talked to the man with baggy clothing, a torn jacket, trampled shoes, and a recycled fountain soda cup. Maybe they were right. Maybe they were wrong. Maybe I am just so jaded to a world of cynicism that I cannot care less anymore.

Or, maybe, I was shown kindness from the wrong crowd once before. The smallest acts of kindness warmed my heart, bent my rules, and made me wish the rest of the world could stop profiling at the drop of a penny.

This is not to say that I never had bad experiences. I've had my fair share of assaults, harassments, and challenging experiences when I've taken those leaps of faith. Based on the level of hurt and trauma that come out of these experiences, I sometimes snap those rules back in place to protect me again. By all means, I hope we are all protecting ourselves. A bad apple does spoil the bunch, and I do carry my own trauma that stops me from being completely selfless to anyone.

How we balance the leaps of faith we take to be kind to strangers while finding appropriate degrees of protection for ourselves is up to us. From there, we need to decide which leaps of faith to take, how far and high we should leap, and when we should turn around. Humans deal with loss at a greater magnitude than gain, and a single bad experience can stay within us longer than a good one. We cannot fight how we are programmed. We should not fight how we are programmed.

At the same time, humans are also programmed to have a bit of kindness in the midst of all that cynicism.

Why does doing an act of kindness for someone else bring so much joy to our hearts when we see them smile? When we watch the evening news, in the midst of breaking headlines about a violent and cruel world, the silver lining comes when we see a miracle happen for a complete stranger that changes their life for the better: a woman is saved from a burning building; a server is given a generous tip that helps her tuition; or a neighborhood rallies money to pay for a neighbor's hospital bill. As cynical as the world is out there, we as humans also want to see it be happy. While this differs within each of us, we cannot deny our heart is lifted, even the tiniest bit, when we see someone's day made a little bit better. Kindness does warm a cold and cynical heart.

Watching the news and waiting for someone else to initiate those acts of kindness as we sit safely within our rules is easy, but taking a leap of faith with an act of kindness can be easy too.

Throughout our busy lives, which only get more and more busy, our attention is demanded from so many directions. Miraculously, we are not overwhelmed with stress on a daily basis. Studies show time and time again that helping others makes people happier. A simple act of kindness for another individual actually carries a surprising amount of self-serving stress relief: we pay less attention to our own problems and ourselves, and more on doing good for others and their problems. This seems small, but it is a relief from our own ongoing problems. We are granted improved emotional functioning that supports our coping mechanisms during stressful situations. Also, we are granted the chance to witness another smile. And that smile alone can be worth it all.

I experienced the kindness of the wrong crowd. I took leaps of faith. I hope you can too.

JULY 13
STRANGERS

11:06 p.m. You asked me today if I just get along easily with everyone I meet. It took me a moment to step back and digest that thought. You're not wrong. I've gotten along extremely well with people right off the bat from meeting them. I know a huge part of this is because of how open I am, or how willing I am to share about experiences I feel most people would be uncomfortable sharing about themselves. I believe there are a few reasons behind this. You could argue it's simply because I've become jaded and desensitized to these problems that I can talk about them so openly and freely with no problem. You could be right. Another reason would be I trust too easily and I am naive and speak too freely with people. I believe this was true at a past point in my life, but not anymore. I feel like the openness

I have now to speak with people comes from a place of being able to come to terms with such emotions, and I am therefore comfortable with them.

Maybe it is naive stupidity to a certain extent. But if it is, I don't have a problem with it.

I think another part of why I'm so open has to do with how I want to be a safe space for others. I want to be someone others recognize as an individual they could talk to about anything and know I would drop anything to be there for them. I hope it's working. I've already had a few people I did not previously know well reach out to me asking for help, and I am grateful individuals like this trust me.

An analysis I gave you was also that when we meet new people, we each have a certain barrier of how much we're willing to tell them as someone new in our lives. Anything past that barrier we save for those who are closer to our hearts. I believe my barrier is simply deeper than others' barriers, and that makes it feel like I'm able to be much closer to others quickly. I'm happy for it, but I know there are those of you out there who think I'm careless. It's something I don't plan to change, though.

DO IT YOURSELF
DO IT FOR
YOURSELF

IDENTITY

#234: *Do it yourself. Do it* for *yourself.*

I look at my driver's license a lot. I did not deserve my driver's license. I failed the driving exam two times, and even on the third try, the examiner shook his head when we pulled back into the parking lot at the end of the course, looked at me, and said, "You know, I am not supposed to pass you because of a left turn you didn't stop at earlier. But I am going to give you this pass since I do not want you to need to retake this entire exam again when you're leaving the state tomorrow."

Thanks, Mr. Examiner. Let's both be glad I am aware of my horrendous driving skills and only use my driver's license when I need legal identification at airport security.

When I look at my driver's license and see eighteen-year-old Emily staring back at me, I wonder how she would feel about herself a few years later. I look at the eighteen-year-old me that did not have an identity, just a driver's license to show for it.

I still think about an analogy my therapist made a few weeks ago. Children who feel safe aren't spared fear. Safe children feel fear but just learn to overcome it knowing there is a parent nearby who makes them feel safe. Like a small trick-or-treater who sees a Halloween decoration and screams, she knows her parents are a few steps away and create that background of safety she can fall back on.

To me this means until our physiological needs and safety needs are met, we do not have room for love, esteem, and self-actualization. Safe children are allowed to reach love, esteem, and self-actualization because they have their safety need met already by their parents.

The ability to develop a sense of identity is a privilege we do not notice. Our brains may have evolved past those of other animals because our survival needs were met much earlier. We are no longer obsessed with survival and instead have the privilege to reach self-actualization. Human society and civilization can be fully accredited to developments of self-identity. As we advance what it means to be human, we explore moral debates and leisurely pleasures. We explore what makes each of us unique and discover what we each stand for, contribute to, and feel fulfilled by.

However, we never just stand up one day and say, "I am no longer obsessed with survival and will be able to pursue my identity now." At least, I hope not. Most of us do not need to think about survival needs anymore. We wake up and know a roof is over our heads and food is available. We use the rest of our brains thinking about how to make a living ("When will my next promotion be?"), develop ourselves ("I have a dance class later tonight"), and pursue leisure activities ("I wonder if my friends will want to watch a movie this Friday evening?"). Most of us do not need to wonder what our identities are, as they are built by how we live out the choices we make.

Most of us do not spend time thinking about what makes up our identities. Our identities simply are. We don't exactly take them for granted, but we do not often question them or need to reconsider. If we were to begin at the very start, how do we piece together an identity?

I spend a decent amount of time thinking about what makes my identity. I was always familiar with the question but never thought much of until I came to the stark realization that I never built mine. I never had the chance to.

I was not a child that grew up feeling safe with my parents or in the household I knew all my life. Since my physiological needs were already met I was searching for that safety. My parents and family were unable to fill that role for me, so I relied on myself. I've relied on myself since I was in middle school, whether financially, mentally, or physically. I did not feel like I had the opportunity to be a child. I was often handed the unfair burdens, weights, and responsibilities of someone older when it was much too early for me. To survive, I had to learn to be an adult first—a *safe* adult. How does one do that without learning how to be a child first? I was both the scared trick-or-treater and the safe adult in the background. Neither knew how to play their role. My life was a constant struggle to fill the shoes of the safe adult I never had but always wanted.

I believe that is why it took me longer than others to develop a sense of identity. I didn't feel safe for so long in my life. I was always on the search for survival, always obsessed with what my future looked like. At the same time, I wanted to be a child, have a childhood, and be able to laugh and play like other children. This duality caused endless conflict in me, eventually developing into a sort of "dual identity" I now realize.

Many people tell me they mistake me as older than I am because of how I carry myself. At the same time, many people also tell me I am one of the most playful, silly, and childlike people they know. These two parts of my identity have always conflicted. Neither is fully who I am, but both are real to me. Both parts are developing at the same time, and both serve me.

I do not think we ever stop building identities for ourselves.

We are always, always learning what to do with ourselves. For each of us, we are surviving in our own ways and living in other ways. What matters is when we notice this and make the active effort to focus our energy on living.

As time progresses, so do our identities. The eighteen-year-old me in my driver's license was living a very different life and a very different identity than the me who is writing this. Both are me, both are parts of my identity, and neither is of lesser importance than the other.

I was recently asked, "If you could change something about your childhood, what would it be?" I laughed because, jeez, where do I start? I would not wish my childhood on anyone. At the same time, I would not wish my childhood to be any different. I crumbled beyond belief sometimes and I stood on the brink of death, but each of these experiences contributed to the identity I currently have. I would not wish for anyone to cry as long and hard as I did, but I also know the thick skin I developed is a product of those experiences. During those moments, I fought to see past the darkness of my days and found the purpose in continuing. My identity was a broken child with hopeless cynicism in her eyes, clawing at anything to keep her alive. I am no longer her, but her identity contributed to the identity I have now: the identity of someone who is healing and hoping to heal others too.

Growing up in a financially unstable household, I have instincts driven by financial anxiety. When I walk in stores, I am disgusted when I notice a voice in my head saying, "Look at this, there's no security systems at the doors. It would be so easy to steal something small that wouldn't hurt this big store." Despite brushing the thoughts away, I am conflicted by the very existence of such thoughts. Am I still the thief I once was if I still think this way? I do not want to be, but maybe I am. Maybe I am not much better.

When we step back and observe ourselves from a removed lens, we see the human brain is so much of a miracle machine that it thinks about itself. An Emily with instincts driven by financial anxiety that tell her how easy it would be to steal exists. An Emily observing the "Emily with stealing instincts" and judging her for having those thoughts also exists. An Emily observing the "Emily with judgment" and telling her to be nicer to herself because we cannot control instincts shaped by how we were raised is there too. Endless Emilys observing the others can be seen and heard as the voices in my head.

So which voice is truly us? Which is our identity?

Something can be said for the fact that we can have thoughts about our thoughts. That, ladies and gentlemen, is called self-awareness, and it is something to be proud of. We do not spend infinite brain power evaluating and reevaluating previous thoughts (can you imagine that headache?), but when we do catch the ones we are less proud of, we've already done something worthy of applause.

We cannot divorce how we were raised from who we are today. We may not like the sound of it, but we are products of our environment more than we may believe. Our environments are baked into our identities whether we like it or not. With our miracle machine brains, though, we can evaluate whether our instincts—the products of our environments—are what we will keep in our identities.

If you already notice instincts you would like to alter, then don't allow yourself to be defined by them. We should be developing our identities around who we want to be, not just who we once were. After all, we do not set goals because we believe we will forever sit at the starting point. We set goals because we have faith that we will be able to reach those goals. We are more defined by the second, third, and fourth thoughts we have than our first instincts, which point to our formative environments more than ourselves.

It can be difficult to give ourselves permission to live if all we know is how to survive. Separating our survival instincts from our living identities is even harder. It's about time we said to ourselves, "Hey, I am no longer obsessed with survival and will be able to pursue my identity now."

JULY 24
9:04 p.m.
PERSONA

Every day, before we start therapy, we have a bit of small talk about how our day was or what our plans are for the weekend. It's very simple, like a conversation you would have with anyone else. I conduct myself like I normally would. But today he said, "Okay, that's public persona Emily. Let's talk with the Emily inside." I had to pause for a moment, wondering if being happy and cheerful was a public persona I displayed for the world outside. I understood from my experiences and jobs that I tended to do well hiding my emotions or putting on a smile even when I didn't feel like it, but did that necessarily mean it was simply a public persona and not a part of me? The two did not need to be mutually exclusive. I asked him, "But public persona me is still me, right?" and he nodded, saying yes, it was definitely a part of me to be able to act and genuinely feel how I was acting despite feeling other more complicated emotions. This meant I was still hiding a personal, darker side of myself. I shouldn't be hiding it. I shouldn't exactly be flaunting it either. I should instead be at a place where I am comfortable with it and don't feel like I hide it anymore. I should be at peace with it.

FIND THE
STRENGTH TO
FORGIVE
YOURSELF WHEN
YOU ARE CLOSEST
TO GIVING UP

FORGIVENESS

#91: Find the strength to forgive yourself when you are closest to giving up.

I used to always say I did not forgive. I used to say it takes a lot for me to get to the point where forgiveness is even necessary, and therefore, not many reach that other side. For those who have, however, I do not forgive.

Does a refusal to forgive mean we are holding on to painful parts of our histories? Some would say so. Some would say until we are able to peacefully give ourselves closure through forgiveness we will always be carrying hurt.

Underneath my stubborn heart, the truth is that my unwillingness to forgive is egocentric. I refuse to forgive a small handful of people in my life, and you will find my own name on that list. It feels like by forgiving them, I give them a piece of myself—a loving piece—that I would rather not share with them. They no longer have liberty to that piece of me. Despite typically being a caring person, forgiveness is where I hit my limits with individuals who cross me.

When it comes to forgiving myself, the same logic applies. I've done much more in my past than I may ever tell anyone— much more that I am ashamed of and will never forgive myself for. Forgiving myself is something I have yet to understand. It feels like giving myself a pardon I did not deserve. I made mistakes, and I should never make them again. I am much more used to holding on to this wrath for myself than telling myself it was okay.

Forgiveness is vulnerability. It means putting down a barrier of grudges held for years to tell someone you forgive them and you no longer hold animosity toward them. Maybe a better way of saying it is that I have a problem being vulnerable with the people who hurt me.

That makes complete sense, right?

The gates of unforgiveness are how I protect my heart from being hurt by the same people who already hurt me once. Because I was once vulnerable with those people, they had the ability to access my heart and hurt me. I learned my lesson and will never let them get close again to cause me pain. That includes myself.

But does forgiveness necessarily mean making yourself vulnerable again?

When we hold on to wrath and distrust for others, we also hold on to hurt. Of course, we need to give ourselves the appropriate time and space to recover from pain, but when we allow ourselves to stand again, does forgiveness mean we open the gates to those who hurt us? Or perhaps forgiveness simply means we walk away from the gates we were watching.

Forgiveness does not mean we let those who hurt us back into our lives with open arms and open hearts. That would be self-destructive and dismissive. Instead, forgiveness means letting go of the hurt we let them sow in us. It means we walk away from the gates keeping them out as a constant reminder of the pain they caused, instead sowing ourselves far from the gates without allowing them to join us.

We do not forgive our abusers just to give more of ourselves in addition to all they already took from us. However, we need to forgive our abusers for us to heal from their wounds and take back what we let them keep for too long. That includes leaving behind the past versions of us at the gates.

How do we even begin to forgive if we have never forgiven?

Forgiveness crosses my mind sometimes. I have become confused with the idea of it. Perhaps the reason I do not forgive others is because I cannot.

If I have not even forgiven myself, I can barely fathom forgiving others. The gate I keep myself at is the widest of all. I will be the one living with myself forever, so I will never be able to run from the past me, whom I keep locked up and can barely look in the eyes.

When I look at Emily from the past, I see a crumpled mess of survival mechanisms harmful for myself and those around me. I see a struggling person who only knew how to be thorny and lash out at the smallest threats. To think I was once her, once that version of me, is a gate I keep in myself. She is not me anymore, and she will not be allowed to come any closer. I look at past Emily and can barely recognize her, much less forgive her.

I wonder whether future Emily is going to look at present Emily and think the same. Will future Emily find present Emily as disgusting as I find the Emily from the past? This is more possible than I would like to admit. The choices I make today may be choices another version of me will refuse to forgive. I am not perfect, and I will make new mistakes that could hurt the people I now care about. I will be learning, and learning comes with experience, but experience barely runs as smoothly as we would like. How much longer will it be before the next version of me finds herself unable to forgive this version? The cycle continues once again, and it will not stop until I put an end to it. So, when I crouch down and look into the eyes of past Emily, I need to see that she was doing her best to survive—just like I am doing now.

Forgive yourself for being hurt by others. Forgive yourself for being hurt by yourself. You were doing the best job you could with the information you had at the time. You did not know what you know now. Blaming yourself for working with what you had, drawing conclusions, and doing what seemed like the safe, right option is pointless. You did your best, and that is all you could do. That was the *best* you could do. Maybe you hurt others along the way. Maybe you hurt yourself. But you were learning like you still are now, and if you can be proud of yourself now, you should be proud of all the versions of you leading you here. They were trying to help. It isn't fair for us not to forgive ourselves when the only crime we committed was trying our best in our own clumsy way with whatever the world handed us.

Forgive yourself to move on from others, to walk away from the hurt they caused your heart. But do not forget you are also someone who needs to be forgiven and moved on from. You have a long road of living with yourself ahead. Leave the baggage behind.

THE HARDEST
THING YOU CAN DO
IS GIVE YOURSELF
THE PERMISSION
TO BECOME WHO
YOU WANT TO BE

PERMISSION

#140: The hardest thing you can do is give yourself the permission to become who you want to be.

I was a master forger by the age of ten—at least, a master forger of my parents' signatures on my permission slips. Like any elementary schooler, I often forgot to ask my parents to give a quick "okay" on the brightly-colored slips I brought home before every field trip. I forgot until the teacher started walking around the room collecting them, and I scribbled a signature worthy of a master forger.

Old habits die hard. I don't mean the forging; I mean the need for permission.

Permission slips never made sense to me. Guardians are asked to give consent for their child to engage in an action, essentially signing away liability: "If my child is hurt during this process, I understood the risks and gave them the permission." What does not make sense to me is asking for the guardian's permission; regardless of whether or not the guardian signs off, the child still has free will about whether they want to engage in the activity. Of course, when we are still young it makes a bit more sense for guardians to guide these choices, but how come after the ripe age of eighteen we are expected to make all these decisions for ourselves? The day we wake up at eighteen, we are given responsibility and maturity we did not have the night before to make choices and bear their consequences. After that arbitrary threshold, we are expected to give ourselves permission. "If I am hurt during this process, I understood the risks."

When do we know we are ready to give ourselves permission? Were we always ready, or will we never be?

*"I used to look up to you and respect you
until you tried to kill yourself."*

"I thought you were smarter than that."

*"Can you drop me off a block away? My parents
don't want me to be seen with you anymore."*

*"She does so much . . . there's no way she's
actually depressed. She does it to herself."*

"What is wrong with you? Are you as messed up as her?"

While I know mental hospitals have not received the best attention in popular media, the treatment I received from my schoolmates was hurtful and reinforced the toxic culture my community bred. After I was released from my involuntary stay, I felt like I was being punished for my disorders. People I once called friends talked behind my back or spoke poison to my face. Parents of family friends called me the "bad seed" they warned their children to stay away from.

It would be an understatement to say my heart hardened as my skin grew tougher.

For as long as I can remember, I was the "golden child" of my family and community. I was the student everyone asked for study advice, the one friends would say was motivational, inspiring, or disturbingly hard-working. Winning awards and leading organizations were normal to me, and I pushed myself to discover new limits. As the expectations from my community piled on, so did my expectations for myself. I was never able to let myself down. I could never disappoint myself or be anything inferior. Nothing was ever good enough, much less the best.

I was raised to show off the picture-perfect life. What everyone saw were top grades, competitive extracurriculars, and a happy, sociable smile. I would be lying if I said this was all a lie. I enjoyed my time outside of the house, spending hours with friends or learning in classrooms. I loved to pretend the pressure building up inside of me and at home did not exist. After all, I was the golden child. And I liked it.

"You're always there to help other people."

"You're so happy-go-lucky. I could never expect to see you cry."

"You're actually the last person I would ever expect to be depressed."

I lived a double life. By day, I was the top student whose life was ideal, and the rest of the community compared themselves to me. By night, I was cutting, screaming, hurling myself against walls, and crying myself to sleep. I did everything I could to keep the two separate from one another. I hoped the uglier, darker part of me could magically disappear one day like it never existed, and no one needed to ever know of it. It was just a phase, right?

I never gave myself permission to be honest about who I was.

My two worlds came crashing down when I returned from the mental hospital back to my high school in the middle of my sophomore year. Everything I built up so diligently for sixteen years melted away. The gig was up.

Neither part of me was fake. I do love being with people who make me laugh and I do love being the reliable friend whose shoulder is always there. I also hurt deeply inside.

Because I so desperately kept these two separated from each other for my whole life, I was never able to fully face the truth of what I was going through. I always told myself I was just going through a phase or that I was just weak compared to everyone else. I grew up with a roof over my head and food on my plate, so I taught myself to believe I did not deserve to feel the dark, heavy feelings I had. I did not know it was not normal for children to be cutting. I desperately wished for the happy, laughing part of me to be the real me, when deep down I know both parts actually were me.

Since I spent all of my childhood development in oblivious disorder, I never gave myself the permission to be okay with my hurt. I refused for so long to believe there was anything wrong with me. I refused to admit the suicidal thoughts I had every week were not healthy. When I was first told at age twelve that I lived in an abusive household, I laughed it off within a few seconds and moved onto talking about my favorite donut flavors. When I was raped at seventeen, I could not let my furious friend call the police even as I was crying to her the next morning, because "rape was a word for people who go through harder experiences." When my therapist first told me at twenty that the trauma within me is more deeply rooted than he had ever seen in anyone my age, I told him I do not suffer from trauma because "my situation wasn't that bad, right?" I could not give myself permission to say I was abused, raped, traumatized, and hurt.

"Emily, when your friends are hurting, you're always the first person to call them or to give them food or offer support. But why are you never there for yourself? Why can you not just say you are hurt?"

"It hurts us to see you not allow yourself to be sad."

"Of course you suffer from trauma. How did you not know that? I've known that for as long as I've known you."

    The first step to healing is recognizing we are in pain. This means recognizing there is something wrong. It does not mean assigning blame or fault to a source causing the hurt. It simply means admitting there is a problem that needs to be fixed. Unfortunately, this is the hardest step to overcome.

    For too long, I could not give myself permission to say I was hurting.

    So I am giving you permission to recognize your hurt.

    I found myself faced with another "permission slip" when I sat in a hospital bed during my first year of college after my anorexia created problems for my heart. Because of my lack of insurance, I politely turned down the doctor's recommendation for inpatient treatment. I lost count of the number of times she approached me with this proposal, a bit more urgent each time. When I was finally looking at her in a hospital bed and still shaking my head, she sighed, shook her head as well, and gave me a liability form. She told me I would need to sign the form to release liability from her. Essentially, I would be saying I received the doctor's recommendation and refused it, so any pending harm or death I may experience was due to my own volition and not medical malpractice. "If I am hurt during this process, I understood the risks."

I signed the permission slip. I didn't forge a signature this time. That signature, signing the responsibility of my well-being back to myself, was both literal and metaphorical.

Giving ourselves permission to say we are hurt is permission to say we are human and we feel pain. This is permission to start healing. Most importantly, however, it is signing your responsibility of your well-being back to yourself.

Only we will be able to take care of ourselves the way we need to. Doctors, nurses, therapists, friends, and family can only provide us with so much care. We need to get ourselves across the finish line, and sometimes we need to be the only ones cheering ourselves on. We are the ones solely responsible for our well-being, and we need to own up to it.

Until you give yourself permission to say you are hurt, the responsibility of your care and healing lies in the hands of everyone but yourself. Give yourself the permission to take back yourself.

Every single one of us will be hurt in our lives. You would be lying if you told me you have never been hurt. You do not need to wonder whether you are "truly hurt" or just a "whiny, dramatic, emotional b-tch" like I did. By questioning whether we are truly hurt, we put our pain into relative terms. I believed I was not truly hurt or traumatized because I knew others with experiences I believed were much, much more horrid than mine. I could not actually be hurt or traumatized. I invalidated my hurt.

Don't invalidate your hurt.

We all experience pain and suffering differently. Your experiences are valid, and the ways you react are natural. The actions you take from such experiences may differ based on your situation, but what does not differ is that you feel feelings unique to yourself. No matter what you go through or experience, no hurt is too large or too small to be a hurt. Give yourself permission to acknowledge, accept, and understand that hurt.

An inability to give ourselves permission to feel the feelings we have comes from many different places. Maybe you do not think you are deserving of those emotions, or you push them down so far in your stomach you no longer see them. The feelings you neglect do not have a permission slip. No one can come along in your life and give you a signature, telling you it is okay to feel how you feel. No one will see the emotions and hurt you hide away if you yourself cannot even see them. You cannot wait for someone else to notice them and tell you what they see. By the time others are able to see your hurt, it may mean the emotions you stashed away are bleeding through and you can no longer hide them. They are bursting at the seams. Do not wait to be a pot boiling over. You need to sign your own permission slips. Only you can do that now.

Give yourself the permission you need to be human.

JULY 7
QUESTIONING MYSELF
9:31 p.m. A serious discussion I had with you and a few other individuals earlier today was about how I was questioning my own depression. Because I completely submitted myself to believing my suicidal thoughts/actions this past month were a melodramatic

search for attention and care, **I started to seriously question the depression I have dealt with for the past eight years.** *Was I truly depressed or was I what my parents always said: someone who just wanted attention? It made me genuinely and completely reconsider whether I was just a fake, overly emotional teenager who was weak and had no control on herself, misplacing a label just to have an excuse.*

Of course, such thoughts spiraled me down darker and darker thoughts of self-hatred. You and a few others dragged me out. Thank you. You made me realize that if this breakup had not happened I would not be questioning this condition I've been suffering from. **You made me realize I was gaslighting myself, and that impostors' syndrome is real.** *Even though I know I will continue to question my own emotions and how valid they really are, thank you for saving me today and giving me a reminder I can revisit in the future. You helped me earn another tool to fight the dark thoughts and dark secrets I've been too scared to ever discuss. I was always scared to ask if my depression was real because I always had my doubts, and by sowing these doubts in those around me I knew it could turn out ugly. Thank you for reassuring me I'm not alone and for allowing me to be vulnerable.*

"You tend to overdo the good things as well. You are just focusing on finding everything you did wrong, but I'm sure that you overdid good things."

JULY 9
ONE MONTH

You told me you thought one month would be too short to make any real change. To be honest, I was rather offended and insulted by how little faith you had in me. I know my disorders and these issues have been a part of me for as long as you have known me. Maybe you thought I was a lost cause. **But it hurt that you didn't have faith in me, especially after I told you I could go up from here.** *I don't think you or I can expect me to move linearly, but I knew I would be moving upward. Maybe you didn't. Maybe you did, and just thought the month wouldn't be enough. Or maybe you just didn't have faith in my potential anymore.*

I don't blame you. I wouldn't have faith in myself either.

JULY 12
TRAUMA

I was told today that I suffer from trauma.

I've never thought of that because I always thought those who have trauma go through much harder experiences in life. But I haven't even told him about what happened in sophomore year of high school when I ended up hospitalized. And he already says I have deep-rooted trauma. It feels strange thinking that I suffer from trauma. I don't feel like I do. I know my past haunts me excessively, but is it really trauma? I told him about everything pre-sophomore year—from all the sexual assaults to my inability to trust my own senses, from the self-harm to the suicide attempts. But from what I believe the worst hasn't been told yet.

Being told I suffer from trauma has made me question so much about my experiences. I made a new friend recently and was telling him about an instance on the Chicago metro when someone kept touching my thighs, and the guy I was with had to stand between us. He told me most girls would be traumatized by an experience like that, yet all I could say was, "Huh, really?" When he asked why I responded like that, I told him I believe I've experienced much worse. I told him about all the assaults I can remember since middle school and he was just . . . speechless. From my perspective, it's not that bad. It's just what happened to me. I can't help but start questioning so many of the experiences I've had like this. I've tossed instances under the rug and not thought about them because I didn't think they were that bad. I can't help but start questioning whether I'm just incredibly desensitized and jaded to such experiences—not just sexual assault, but also emotional abuse, self-deprecation, etc. **I can't help but wonder how many more experiences I've had that I can't even remember because I've just shut them away. Were these self-defense mechanisms I've developed for myself as a hardened shell against the worst experiences? I can't know what I don't know.**

I think I'm realizing this journal's greatest value to me is that it allows me to process my emotions outside of my head, instead of alone as I always have.

When we started therapy today, I said, "Sorry I was late" because I was a minute late. He told me the fact that I say sorry so frequently and often discount my experiences or emotions when I recall my experiences shows how deeply rooted my trauma has become. Is it okay to believe him? I still cannot help but feel like my experiences are not bad enough to warrant the label of trauma. **Trauma happens to those who go through wars in life. I've only gone through battles.**

When I said I felt I was forced to grow up too quickly, that I never had the chance to develop my childhood, you said:

"Yes, you did. You didn't get to learn to recover after hurt."

YOU DO NOT NEED
TO KNOW WHY
YOU ARE FILLED
WITH HOPE JUST
YET

HOPE

#278: You do not need to know why you are filled with hope just yet.

Is there a word for the fear of hope?

I do not think it is doubt. Doubt means there is hesitation, but it does not show a lack of hope. One can be both hopeful and doubtful at the same time. Despair does not seem to fit either. Despair is an absence of hope, not necessarily the opposite. To simply not be filled with hope does not show the opposite of hope, just a lack.

Hope is having positive expectations of the future. It means optimistic expectations for what is to come and believing the best will come. Hope is a set of future events we not only would like to see but are expecting to see. With hope, we look for positive outcomes and hold our breath in excited anticipation.

Hope can truly uplift a soul. It can also drive a soul to utter disappointment. Hope is sharp at its edges and should be handled with care.

This was the first year I ever felt hope. When I was sitting at my desk one evening, I was hit with the realization that I felt hope for the first time in my life. However, instead of joyous gratitude, realization brought me unrivaled levels of fear and anxiety.

My fear of hope begins with a fear of the unknown. As someone with borderline personality disorder, accepting gray space is difficult and I need defined answers. This began when I grew up as a reserved child in a household that was more often quarrelsome than it was peaceful. By keeping my senses alert and picking up on every hint, I was able to assess situations and decide how I should act. I listened to every single word thrown, every single plate shattered against a wall, and every single footstep on every single stair. I felt a certain level of panic arise when, in the midst of a fight, I heard sudden silence. Aside from the possibility that some event caused silence to hang in the air, I became restless in my head. I wondered if I missed something or if something happened but I was not able to predict it. I was unable to react.

Even now, I have difficulty being in situations where I do not know everything. During social events, I like to be more quiet than talkative so I can watch everyone's behaviors and draw conclusions about how to best act with them. I try to gather as much information as possible with as little as possible left unknown.

What is so bad about the unknown? Well, the unknown is simply that: unknown. Its results are unpredictable and can't be reacted to in advance. Unknown situations seem infinitely so. They lack answers and the opportunity to be observed.

Since unknowns cannot be predicted or identified, they could be subjectively good or bad. Just as much chance exists for the unknown to be what you want as it does for the unknown to be what you don't want. Part of the thrill of the unknown is never knowing what lies in it.

Paired with my pessimism, the unknown simply becomes a field day of despair. Due to the lack of information surrounding the unknown, my brain defaults to a hopeless attitude. It has a track record of being disappointed when anticipated expectations fail to happen, so to protect itself from feeling the disappointment again, my brain approaches the world with a "guilty until proven innocent" attitude. Anything unanswered defaults to whatever the worst-case scenario can be. That way, regardless of the outcome, it will always at least be better than what was expected. It would never touch hope because it is trying to protect itself.

Carrying hope means carrying expectations and anticipating that being optimistic is worth the possible letdowns. It means willingness to put yourself at risk when what is hoped for does not play out accordingly. It means vulnerability and an understanding that hope is simply hope—not a greater guarantee of the outcome we would like.

Finding out I was carrying hope was a scary moment. I felt color drain from my face when I felt hopeful for the upcoming year, hopeful for the progress I would be making, and hopeful for the good memories I could be creating. I found that amid all that hope, a stronger feeling was present—fear.

Perhaps fear is the fear of hope.

I feared disappointment. I feared beating myself up a year later when I would not be able to fulfill all I was hopeful for. I feared hurting myself, my expectations, and my self-esteem when the hope I had shattered as all of reality eventually came brutally crashing down.

The fear was paralyzing. I was unable to move as I sat in a cold sweat, playing through every single scenario that could happen if my hopes were not fulfilled. I thought about the weight of disappointment. I felt it starting to press down upon me until I was nearly suffocated by my own fear of hope.

Hope means positive expectations, yet expectations are just that. More expectations will not make a hypothetical future more likely to happen but simply make the height from which we can come crashing down even higher. The more hope exists, the more room there is for disappointment. And for me, disappointment was to be avoided at all costs.

At the same time, I found myself desperately wishing I could hope. I did not want to trap myself in a vacuum of constant, unrelenting anxiety that paralyzed me from taking steps forward anymore. I did not want to go into every situation with a "guilty until proven innocent" outlook. That made me more eager to look for evidence proving the former than the latter. I did not want to allow myself to continue living in constant search of proof that the world was a disappointing place to be in, but I also did not know how to have expectations without fearing the fall from them.

Overcoming the fear of falling from hope is the hardest step to reaching hope. How wonderful it would be to build resilience so, when you do fall, you do not reach the devastating depths of disappointment. Instead, you land softly, brush the dust from your knees, stand straight, and look up at hope again. And then, when you are ready, you can again begin climbing the ladder of expectations toward hope.

I used to think people who were hopeful were incredibly stupid and naive. Unlike in TV shows, results do not change the more we hope for their outcome. Actions can be taken to swing the compass of fate, but there always comes a point when all that can be done is to watch chance take its course. When you reach that point, you choose to hope or to not. If the outcome is less than ideal, the hopes that were held are unfulfilled and you fall down the height of your hope. How stupid it was to watch people climb up that ladder again and again to reach hope, witness an unfulfilling outcome, fall back down, and climb once more. How naive they were to keep looking up when, according to statistics, the chances of a different outcome grew more and more bleak each time it failed to show up. How I pitied watching their climbs and falls from the same ladders and heights.

Yet the difference between them and me was that I was forever on the ground. To be safe, I never climbed up a ladder of hope. I did not carry their scars and bruises from each fall, but I also never gave hope a chance. While very few people in my life ever did successfully have a hope fulfilled, the fact of the matter is they still existed, and they fulfilled a hope because they had a hope. They climbed up a ladder, reached the top against all odds, and their hope was fulfilled because they stayed up there. Meanwhile, I remained safely unharmed down on the ground, never giving myself the chance to reach heights.

Mathematical theories attempt to calculate the probabilities of events from the most random to the most sequential. Each have their own conclusions, and each have their own chances of success. Regardless of these probabilities, the safest option is to never have hope—to never be hurt, and to never take the risks. The riskiest option is to have hope, to keep climbing ladders until you manage to reach the top and find what you are looking for. Playing with odds may mean one will be hurt more often than they will be happy, but the greatest difference is that only by playing with odds will we even have the chance to be happy.

Only by playing with hope will we have the chance to look up instead of forever seeing only at ground level.

JULY 7

7:03 p.m. I don't feel like eating at all, and not even from anorexia. I don't feel hungry. I've been awake for twenty-one hours and have only had one meal. I just finished dinner. Pretending everything is okay and shoving food in your mouth is strange. Nothing tastes good. The more I ate the more I wanted to throw up. I didn't even eat a lot—maybe even a bit less than my normal meal portion. I just wanted to throw up. Not even because of anorexia—I just physically felt nausea while eating.

After dinner I tried to throw up. I felt so sick I immediately ran to the toilet. But nothing came out. I just cried in front of the toilet.

It's an awful feeling. I feel crumpled.

7:34 p.m. I feel so sick. Physically sick. Tired and nauseous, but nothing I can do to help myself feel better is working.

SICK

7:35 p.m. I'm trying to stay positive, trying to keep my head up. But it's hard when my body doesn't seem to even want to stay up, even after I thought I had dealt with my physical disorders. Is it anemia again? I doubt it. That feels like an excuse.

7:43 p.m. Today I learned many lessons from my friends. These are lessons I would have said were easy and should be automatically understood, but obviously I didn't understand them until today. Maybe I still don't. I'm still learning.

Accepting time for grieving is healthy.

Do what you need to give yourself closure. Fight yourself.

Be open-minded, seriously. Don't just think you are. Be open to ideas others have.

7:50 p.m. My mood has been fluctuating all day—all, all day. Sometimes I think things will be okay. But then other times I'm completely crumpled and broken and crying.

But the difference between today and last week is that even though I am broken, I have hope. The hope isn't strong enough, but I want to have faith in that hope. I want to.

JULY 8

2:14 p.m. I woke up this morning and I was hit with a wave of anxiety and blame and guilt. Waking up is so painful now. The pain numbs during the day as I do work and try to ignore it, yet I know it's there. It just eats and eats at me.

I'm going to try to nap.

5:25 p.m. Anxiety really does hit hardest when I wake up. I was able to nap for two hours but spent an hour thinking and regretting all I did to you. I'm so sorry you had to be with me for so long. The more I think about how I became suicidal with my self-control still intact continues to haunt me and makes me wonder how much of it I could have stopped before it hurt you. I cannot help but believe I could have stopped a lot.

It feels like a giant rock in my stomach. It weighs me down and I feel no desire, no motivation to do anything.

5:34 p.m. Yesterday I kept thinking if I were to get better soon, I wanted to start moving toward self-care and start creating plans for myself. Then the anxiety truck hit me this morning and the motivation all disappeared. If you asked me what it feels like, it feels like depression. It feels like an unwillingness to move or to do anything, even things I was previously looking forward to.

FUTILITY

I don't feel motivated at all to be happier. I don't see why I should try to make myself happier when I know the drop down will only be that much deeper. We'll always be disappointed at one point or another. We'll always have these cycles of happiness and disappointment. I've always felt the times of disappointment completely nullify the happiness I've accumulated. I'm just too exhausted to try anymore. I'm just too tired to do anything at all.

However, I recognize this is a problem that also addresses the core of my depression. Not just recently but always. I'm not motivated to find or make my own happiness.

My happiness has always depended on the people around me. I was happy when my friends were happy. But my sadness and darker times come from myself, and I push myself deeper down. What lifts me up has never been myself but my friends. Because I don't want to even lift myself up. I don't feel motivated to be happy. **I want to fix it, but that want to fix it is not stronger than my sense of futility and defeat already.**

At the lowest point of today I felt the will to live walk away from me. It didn't run. It walked.

12:36 a.m. You asked how I could still be laughing and joking even after going through the emotions that I did. I don't know either, **but it's better to feel the joy in the moment and save the sadness for another time, right?**

AUGUST 30
HOPE

1:21 p.m. "I think that's what's beautiful about hope. You have no other choice but to hope, so you might as well have all hope in hope."

A few months ago, I never would have been able to say this to someone. But it's something I've since learned, and it's completely changed my life. I've been more positive, more optimistic, and more hopeful since. When I look at myself previously, it's hard to believe I used to live in so much darkness, feeding my own negativity with my thoughts. Even looking at the start of this journal I saw so much darkness in me.

At the very least, I'm proud of myself.

PART IV

A LETTER

An open letter to younger me, on the edge.

It's hard to know where to begin and even harder to know where to end. But your story is nowhere near over if you make every day a new start. So please keep going. Keep reading your story back to yourself when you lose the next chapter, keep writing, and keep turning the pages.

When you are twelve, you'll learn what it means to be overwhelmed by all that is on your little shoulders. You'll learn what self-harm feels like, that addicting relief of a cold blade dragging against warm skin. You'll lose faith in the community you know, you'll break apart and crumble, and you'll throw away pieces of yourself in a deep, deep darkness you think is "only a phase." You'll have your first experience of sexual assault. You'll start learning what distrust tastes like and forget what it means to have friends. You'll think you're weak against the world, that you're a coward, and that you're too naive and immature to feel the feelings that overwhelmed you for so long. You'll let go of hope. You'll have your first suicide attempt.

When you are sixteen, you'll learn what it means to throw yourself away. Regularly, you'll run away from the house where loud noises and anger haunt you. You'll smile and pretend everything is okay because that's what everyone expects. You'll keep it up. You'll be really good at it, actually. You'll be diagnosed. You'll see therapy and you'll leave therapy. You'll pretend to be "normal," and you'll make sure the rest of the world never hears about how ugly and twisted you are inside. You'll be really good at all of it. You'll experience sexual assault again. You'll have your fourth suicide attempt. You'll wake up in a mental hospital in an unknown bed in an unknown room. You'll return to school after a few weeks, only to have that facade shattered when your entire being is questioned by the darkness that is now you. You'll come closer to death than you admit.

When you are eighteen, you'll learn what it means to give yourself up for death. You'll write more suicide notes than you can count. You'll lose sight of what happiness feels like and what memories with friends are supposed to look like. You'll give up so many of your childhood and teenage experiences because nothing feels fun anymore. You'll stop feeling anything when you're assaulted again. You'll fail to even realize you've been assaulted. You'll start to find comfort in distractions, in eating disorders and burnouts. You'll enjoy independence. No one will notice your self-harm anymore. You'll end up in the ER again on your birthday, but you'll forget to blink an eye when you're told you could die at any moment as a consequence of your actions. You'll say hello to death a second time.

When you are twenty, you'll learn what it means to lose sight of a future. You'll have heartbreak and you'll reach rock bottom again. You'll lose everything you've worked for your whole life, including those you thought would be lifelong partners. You'll be desensitized to the world's darkest hours, and you'll be blind to your own trauma. You'll try to feel better by recklessly harming your body and heart. You'll lose count of how many times you've tried to kill yourself.

Yet, little one, when you are twenty, you'll also learn to live again. You'll learn what love feels like, and you'll have the love of not only those around you, but also those whose lives have touched yours. You'll learn what gratitude feels like and what it means to appreciate and be grateful for all we have, even in the smallest joys. You'll learn what trust feels like, and you'll start to have faith again in the world and its workings and possibilities. You'll have coworkers and friends who will become family. You'll have a new religion to remind you of hope in dark hours. You'll have a journal to record your emotions. You'll learn to be vulnerable again against a hardened world and your own hardened heart. You'll have a therapist. You'll learn more about yourself and your past than you were previously comfortable with. You'll have a mirror in your room lined with memories and photos of those you love so you can look at your reflection again with a smile. You'll have music you enjoy jamming out and losing yourself to, learning what it means to live in the moment. You'll make memories and friends in places you never expected and you'll learn to treasure these relationships more than ever. You'll be grateful you kept going. You'll have crazy ambitions, crazy memories, and goals. You'll want to recover and live again.

You'll know that life, from here on, is not completely damage-proof. You're going to fall again. You're going to struggle with your past as you grow toward a future. You'll still find it impossible to know what it means to love yourself. You'll have nights when crying happens more than sleep. You won't know how much there is left to recover of yourself, but you'll commit to living again. You won't know what hardships life may throw in your path again, but you'll know you're so much stronger now—so, so much stronger.

So much can change in you within a day, a month, a year, or a lifetime. When you are twelve, sixteen, and eighteen, you will never be able to fathom where you'll be at twenty. When you are twenty-two, twenty-four, and thirty, you will be in places that you, at twenty, may be unfamiliar with but know is a better place. You won't know what you don't know. You won't know what happiness you could find in the future, so you can't give up yet.

So please, step away from the edge. Try just one more time. Because I promise on my life, little one, you will be happy.

ACKNOWLEDGMENTS

Thank you for reading this book to its end. It nearly did not happen and was rewritten more times than I will count. Thank you for being part of it.

To the people in my life who stood by me through trial and terror, you are the reason I am still alive and kicking and somehow published. You raised a broken child into a bandaged, stumbling, but still standing adult. You saved a life.

To the team at New Degree Press, thank you for providing a platform and believing in my book. You are all making miracles happen in this world.

This book was made possible by a community of people who may not know me but believed in me enough to support or preorder my book. You are wonderful and a part of this book's existence.

And to my family: thank you for bringing me into this world and into a life I no longer regret.